MW00837046

How Colleges Use Data

How Colleges Use Data

Jonathan S. Gagliardi

Johns Hopkins University Press · *Baltimore*

© 2022 Johns Hopkins University Press
All rights reserved. Published 2022
Printed in the United States of America on acid-free paper
9 8 7 6 5 4 3 2 1

Johns Hopkins University Press
2715 North Charles Street
Baltimore, Maryland 21218
www.press.jhu.edu

Library of Congress Cataloging-in-Publication Data

Names: Gagliardi, Jonathan S., author.
Title: How colleges use data / Jonathan S. Gagliardi.
Description: Baltimore : Johns Hopkins University Press, 2022. | Series: Higher
    ed leadership essentials | Includes bibliographical references and index.
Identifiers: LCCN 2022005127 | ISBN 9781421445199 (paperback) |
    ISBN 9781421445205 (ebook)
Subjects: LCSH: Universities and colleges—United States—Administration—Data
    processing. | Education, Higher—Research—United States—Data processing. |
    Education, Higher—Research—United States—Statistical methods.
Classification: LCC LB2341 .G255 2022 | DDC 378.1/010973—dc23/eng/20220317
LC record available at https://lccn.loc.gov/2022005127

A catalog record for this book is available from the British Library.

*Special discounts are available for bulk purchases of this book. For more information,
please contact Special Sales at specialsales@jh.edu.*

For my family and friends, old and new, and Winnie

Contents

Preface

At the start of this decade, colleges and universities looked much as they had for years, if not centuries. Campuses bustled with students and staff, eagerly engaging in preparations for the year ahead despite often unenviable conditions, such as long lines at the registrar and stubborn account holds, which left everyone desiring a more seamless experience. Faculty, with some exceptions, stood before their students in the traditional lecture style and labored away in their labs, seeking the next discovery or creation that would push the frontiers of knowledge forward. Deans and department chairs constantly monitored their school and program enrollments as they competed for resources and bragging rights. Proud building and administration crews beautified grounds and made repairs to buildings. Tucked away in the top floor of an administrative building, senior campus leaders worked to strike a balance between extinguishing the many fires lit throughout the day and planning, with cautious optimism, for a brighter future.

That familiar picture would quickly vanish when the world was turned upside down by the emergence of a global pandemic. On January 20, 2020, the first patient in the United States was diagnosed with COVID-19. Society was tragically slow to shutter up, and sadly, roughly one million Americans were lost at the time of this writing. The pandemic triggered an economic downturn that was far worse than the Great Recession of 2008-2009 and was exceeded only by the Great Depression. Millions were left without work as businesses closed indefinitely. As colleges and universities closed, some observers thought were finally receiving their comeuppance after decades of ignoring flashing red lights that warned of mounting social, political, economic, and technological pressures.

Despite myriad hardships in recent years, there is a great deal for colleges and universities to be proud of. During a decade of uncertainty, higher education has risen to the occasion, proving many naysayers wrong. Entire university systems mobilized seemingly overnight to shift almost all their academic programs and services online while also battling the digital divide. Colleges found ways to serve as drive-through testing sites while keeping food banks open and serving their communities. Faculty kept teaching, advisors kept advising, and students kept learning. Under normal circumstances, these achievements would be considered inspirational.

However, these are anything but normal times, and what has transpired has led US higher education to a seminal moment, albeit in an unexpected way. Things once thought impossible—such as the rapid digital transformation of academic programs and the realignment of student services with the needs of contemporary students—are now happening, guided by the steady hands of presidents and senior campus leaders. Since the pandemic, colleges and universities have taken more steps toward modernization than in the years and perhaps decades prior. A great deal of innovation and progress has been made. It is important to ensure that the best of it takes root over the course of the next decade.

It is also true that the major challenges that existed prior to the global crisis remain. The financial model that most colleges and universities use is in a state of disrepair. More needs to be done to ensure that students, faculty, and staff can effectively learn, teach, and serve across multiple modalities. The partnership between government, business, society, and colleges needs to be renewed. Science, the arts, and basic research have been ignored for too long.

In some cases, challenges have been magnified. The need to remove persistent and inequitable access and outcomes has been exposed as one of the great moral imperatives of our time, particularly in the aftermath of civil unrest in response to police violence against people of color. These equity gaps are just some of the many indicators of social injustice, and if higher education is truly to be the great equalizer, then colleges and universities must do everything within their power to undo centuries of mistreatment. We cannot be complicit in perpetuating an unjust system of social, political, and economic constructs that marginalize, oppress, and entangle people of color and the poor. We can recommit to serving as engines of equity and opportunity and as stewards of place. There are reasons to believe that colleges and universities are up to the task. Presidents and senior campus leaders are coming to realize that using data and analytics will make the job easier.

Colleges can use data to successfully fulfill their mission, vision, and values, even in the face of unprecedented adversity. The effective and ethical use of data and analytics can simultaneously improve the academic and non-academic experience in ways that promote student success, equity, and institutional sustainability.

This book was written to help college and university leaders understand the rapidly accelerating analytics revolution in higher education that can empower them to tap into the potential of a growing sea of data. Using data analytics will help leaders steer their institutions effectively in what is sure to be a decade of innovation and organizational transformation. The book focuses on the relationship between campus executives and data, as little literature addresses this relatively new intersection. Much of the work that follows is based on personal experiences and the guidance of mentors and colleagues.

Colleges and universities have a major role to play in helping a new world take shape for the benefit of all people. In many ways, their traditional roles as agents of upward mobility and champions of social justice are more indispensable than ever before. What is new are the tools and strategies that presidents and senior campus leaders have at their disposal to fulfill these roles. Leading the creation of a culture of evidence by harnessing the analytics revolution is perhaps their best strategy for answering the call for change.

This time is a rare moment where fate, circumstance, and inconceivable shifts in how colleges fulfill their mission are offering senior campus leaders a sudden but fleeting chance to cement hard-won institutional changes. If data and analytics are properly and effectively mobilized, they can help leaders do so successfully.

Acknowledgments

My appreciation is extended to Johns Hopkins University Press and to editorial director Greg Britton, who during a chance conversation saw potential in exploring the intersection of the analytics revolution and higher education leadership. I would also like to acknowledge the efforts of Sarah Fuller Klyberg, who patiently supported the refinement of this book.

To my colleagues who offered their insights about this work and shaped my views over time, thank you. José Luis Cruz, Jason E. Lane, Nancy L. Zimpher, Rebecca Martin, Louis Soares, Lorelle Espinosa, Daniel Lemons, Gladys Maldoon, Edward Sullivan, Amelia Parnell, Gina Johnson, Christine Keller, Jane Wellman, Karen Crowe, Lyndsay Wayt, Mamie Voight, Konrad Mugglestone, Amanda Janice Roberson, Rick Staisloff, Colin Chellman, David Troutman, and Cheryl Littman, your wisdom and experience helped to make this book possible and will help advance our shared understanding of a topic that is still emerging.

I also want to express my heartfelt gratitude to my family for their unconditional support and inspiration. I am ever grateful to my parents, JoAnn and Anthony, who lovingly encouraged my appreciation for higher education from the time I was very young.

How Colleges Use Data

Chapter 1

The Evidence Imperative

The Analytics Revolution

In 2012, the Pew Research Center issued a report that focused on imagining what a data-fueled future might look like in 2020.[1] As part of the report, a panel of digital stakeholders was asked to weigh in on whether the net effects of big data and analytics, would be positive or negative. The panel was split. Some saw unlimited opportunities to use big data and analytics to improve commerce, connect the world, strengthen education, promote equity, and combat poverty, crime, climate change, and disease. Others warned that governments, the private sector, and members of society could wield big data and analytics as tools of power, oppression, and inequity.

Both perspectives have proven to be true in the decade since the report. The analytics revolution has been used in helpful and harmful ways. This dual outcome has been made possible by the exponential growth of available data and advances in technology.

By early 2021, an estimated 64.2% of the global population was using the internet.[2] Each day, humans create 2.5 quintillion bytes of data. At the beginning of 2020, the amount of data that existed was 44 zettabytes, a total that was forty times more than the number of stars in the observable universe.[3] By 2025, it is estimated that there will be 75 billion Internet of Things devices.[4] Advances in cloud-based storage and integration of data, analytics, artificial intelligence, automation, and machine learning are accelerating these trends.[5] At the same time, barriers to entry such as cost and technical infrastructure have diminished, in part because the big data and analytics sector has grown rapidly in recent years. By 2022, the market for big data and business is expected to generate revenue of $274.3 billion, which represents double-digit annual growth since 2019.[6] The end result is greater democratization of data and broader adoption of analytics among people and organizations.

Big data and the analytics revolution have reached a state of ubiquity that affects our daily lives in profound and beneficial ways that are both subtle and unsubtle. For example, the explosion of smartphones and mobile applications and the maturation of the Global Positioning System (GPS) have transformed how we travel locally (by helping us avoid a traffic jam on the way to work) and globally (through enhanced booking and instantly customized recommendations for travel experiences and destinations). For many people, weekly trips to the market or hardware store have been replaced with store-to-door deliveries based on analyses of historical purchases and consumer preferences. Cities now use big data to improve public transportation. Greener energy grids, improved healthcare, healthier lifestyles, and countless other facets of our lives have been improved as a result of this phenomenon.[7]

There are also plenty of risks associated with the proliferation of big data and the analytics revolution. As Cathy O'Neil noted in her groundbreaking work, the emergence of big data, artificial intelligence, and machine learning have introduced innumerable threats to the health and well-being of individuals and society. Mathematical models, which O'Neil refers to as weapons of math destruction (WMDs), that many view as miraculous also pose threats to equity and social justice in the areas of health care, housing, criminal justice, and yes, education.[8] These WMDs can inflict a great deal of damage. The Data Harm Record, a project of the Data Justice Lab at Cardiff University, provides a running record of data misuse, broadly characterizing abuses of data in a number of ways.[9] Populations can be targeted based on vulnerability in a process that amounts to a sort of "algorithmic profiling."[10] Personal information can be misused to ascribe a value to individuals, a practice credit card companies use to determine credit worthiness. Some countries use big data to surveil, reward, and punish its citizens; China's facial recognition and artificial intelligence system is an example.[11] Big data and the analytics revolution have also been used to discriminate. Data breaches have been used to commit identity theft, among other crimes. In the United States, the analytics revolution has intensified social and political division by creating invisible filters that divide the public and undermine democracy through the targeted distribution of fake news. Big data and the analytics revolution have been used to magnify the best and worst in humanity and society. It is worth remembering that a tool is an object that cannot be blamed for the way it is used. The user is ultimately responsible for using a tool for good or bad.

The Pew Research report pointed out that "humans seem to think they know more than they actually know, but despite all of our flaws, looking at the big picture usually helps."[12] So even if people have a vision of a more perfect world shaped by the effective and ethical use of big data and the analytics revolution, achieving that vision requires both a strategy for using data well and the skills and competencies that can turn ideas into reality. By and large, society is not there yet. Many organizations are falling short in their efforts to become data informed because they lack the strategies, infrastructure, resources, culture, and skills do so.[13] The same rings true of the current state of big data and analytics in US higher education. Given how high the stakes are, this situation needs to change.

An Emerging Need to Use Analytics

Even before the emergence of COVID-19 in the spring of 2020, US higher education was facing an unprecedented evidence imperative. Before the pandemic, colleges and universities were already dealing with troublesome enrollment trends, an increasingly hostile political landscape, the continued destabilization of state funding, and growing public doubt about the benefits of higher education for individuals and society.

Higher education has been facing a national enrollment decline. Annual undergraduate enrollments fell by 1.25 million students, or 5 percentage points, across all institutions of higher education from the 2014-15 to the 2018-19 academic years.[14] This pattern is in keeping with projections that the nation will produce fewer high school graduates until 2023. These trends are expected to persist longer in the Northeast and Midwest, which by 2030 are expected to experience declines in the number of high school graduates of 11 and 12 percentage points from 2013 levels, respectively.[15] Since 2016, changes in federal policy have also had a chilling effect on international enrollments, an important source of revenue for colleges and talent for our nation.

The undergraduate student population has become more diverse over time, largely driven by the growth of Latinx enrollment.[16] The proportion of undergraduate students who identify as a race or ethnicity other than white increased from 29% in 1995-96 to 47% in 2015-16.[17] The share of undergraduates in poverty has also grown during this time frame, from 20% to 31%.[18] This compositional shift in undergraduate enrollments has not been spread evenly; the bulk has occurred at public two-year colleges and the least-selective four-year colleges and universities.

Weaker student supports at these institutions may diminish these students' chances for success.[19]

The political climate has grown more hostile to higher education. Opposition comes from across the ideological spectrum. Declining support for colleges and universities among Republicans has been well documented in recent years, and there are signs that more people share that attitude regardless of their beliefs.[20] Recent scandals in undergraduate admissions and data regarding the ability—or inability—of colleges to propel underprivileged students up the economic ladder have generated uncharacteristically harsh criticism from Democrats and independents.[21]

The long-term trend of wavering state support also continues. Before the pandemic, per-student funding for higher education in forty-three states was still below 2008 pre-recession levels. Nationally, educational appropriations remained 8.7% below pre-recession levels.[22] This means that students now carry a greater share of the burden of paying for college. By 2021, the share of institutional revenues that came from student tuition had risen to 46.9%, up from 20.9% in 1980.[23] Student tuition is expected to surpass 50% of institutional revenues in the near future, even as a growing share of the college-going population comes from low-income groups.[24] As a result, the affordability problem and issues related to inequity in higher education could worsen, which would further erode public faith in the uplifting power of a college degree.

Two of the most visible features of these converging crises are rampant inefficiency and inequity, which are in some way already a challenge for nearly all institutions. The reality is that fewer than six in ten college students (58.3%) graduate in six years. Simply put, students pay for a lot of education that does not result in a degree. This is particularly true for students who stand to derive the greatest value from earning a degree. Despite promising gains in completion rates among Black and Latinx students, Asian and white students remain far more likely to complete their degree programs.[25] Completion gaps also exist based on income, gender, the intersection of race and gender, and enrollment intensity.[26]

The affordability crunch, fueled in part by the continued decline of state funding, is likely to get bigger. Over the last three decades, the incomes of American families in the lowest quintile grew at a rate that was 5.5 times slower (8%) than that of families in the highest quintile (46%).[27] Simultaneously, average tuition and fees tripled at four-year public institutions and doubled at public two-year and private not-for-profit four-year institutions.[28] If institutions are unable address these disparities, more students from low-income and/or historically disadvantaged backgrounds will struggle to earn a degree with less financial aid and higher tuition. This combination of circumstances could lead to a vicious cycle of declining effectiveness and public confidence.

Nearly all of these trends are likely to intensify—particularly given the effects of the pandemic, heightened political polarization, growing racial and economic inequity, and the social unrest caused by the convergence of these crises with systemic racism and discrimination—unless colleges and universities reimagine who they serve and how they serve them without giving up their hallmark distinctiveness and quality. This task will be difficult, given that social, political, economic, and technological changes have begun to undermine the business and financial models of colleges and universities. However, it is not impossible, and many institutions of higher education have responded to this series of crises by experimenting and innovating. One of the most notable examples of this innovation has been the successful engagement by colleges and universities nationwide with big data and the analytics revolution.

An Evidence-Based Path Forward

The conversation around the use of data in higher education is not new. The federal government has collected data for enrollment, earned degrees conferred, and faculty since 1869-70,[29] and functions now carried out by offices of institutional research have existed for at least as long. Use of the Integrated Postsecondary Education Data System began in 1985-86 with the institutional characteristics survey and has continued to evolve to include information such as enrollment, student demographic and success data, degrees, finance, employee, and library data, for example.[30] Since at least 1972 the National Science Foundation has collected data on the research and development activities of higher education institutions, and Delaware Cost Study has collected data annually for thirty years from more than 700 institutions in order to promote the measurement of instructional costs and productivity.[31]

Since the late 2000s, interest in data use in higher education has evolved rapidly, first coalescing around student success, equity, and institutional finance. Organizations such as the Education Trust partnered with the National Association of System Heads to convene the Access to Success Network, a group of systems focused on using data to promote student success and equity. In the period 2007 to 2012, the Delta Project on Postsecondary Costs, Productivity, and Accountability worked to improve affordability by focusing on higher education finance data. Beginning around 2010, the integration of unemployment insurance records and tax data with completion data became more mainstream. This practice introduced better and more precise data on postgraduate outcomes, giving colleges and universities a glimpse (albeit a limited one) into what happens after students graduate. For the first time, the stars had aligned to form a constellation of data that colleges and universities could use to understand what they did well and what they could do better.

The higher education community began to use its broadening understanding of quantitative and qualitative data to identify bright spots in what institutions were doing to improve, especially in areas related to student success and equity. As it turned out, many were using data in both routine and innovative ways. This process of discovery unearthed challenges related to data infrastructure, analytics capacity, and culture, which led to a burst of intense focus on the potential of effective institutional research as one key to institutional transformation. It was at this point that the higher education community's understanding of how to use data effectively began to rapidly increase.

Momentum around using data accelerated when stories emerged of colleges and universities completely transforming themselves by harnessing big data and the analytics revolution. Georgia State University and Florida State University increased their graduation rates by more than 20 percentage points while making substantial progress toward narrowing or eliminating equity gaps. Others, such as Indian River State University, a community college in Florida, used data to achieve graduation rates, transfer rates, and bachelor's attainment rates that are well above national averages. Numerous other campuses have improved student success by significantly increasing completion rates for credentials and degrees, substantially reducing and/or eliminating equity gaps, and lowering barriers to access by recalibrating admissions standards in ways that open doors and change lives. One key to these stories was an institutional commitment to creating a culture and infrastructure that can deliver timely, accurate, relevant, and integrated data. As one might imagine, these reports of success drew national interest, whetting the appetite of college and university leaders for using data.

Not a Magic Pill

Many campus leaders would like to harness the analytics revolution so they can fundamentally transform their institutions. Evidence of this ambition is in the strategic plans of many colleges and universities from the last ten years. They are filled with goals and strategies for using data more effectively or for building a best-in-class analytics infrastructure. The fact that many campus leaders have turned to analytics to promote student success, equity, and sustainability across multiple dimensions is promising. However, the efforts of campus administrators to making the big shift from leading with instincts, wisdom, and policy-based evidence to leading with evidence-based policy can fall short. The entry costs of effective data use are high from a monetary perspective and—perhaps more important—from the perspectives of campus cultures and politics. When coupled with the reality of shortening presidential tenures, some senior leaders choose not to engage in such efforts, opting instead to continue their careers at institutions that secondary and tertiary measures, access to resources, and political support suggest are primed to do well and gain recognition.

To build a lasting culture of evidence, senior campus leaders need to do more than pay lip service to big data and the analytics revolution. They must back it up with actions and resources that connect data across the diverse and siloed functions of their institutions. Evidence suggests that more needs to be done in that area. The most recent American College President Study revealed that presidents saw assessment of student learning, student success, graduation, equity, and strategic finance as increasingly important, but their perception of the necessity of using institutional research or evidence to inform decision-making lagged substantially.[32] Some of the consequences of this disconnect include data that remains siloed by functional area, the perception that data are used for punitive purposes or to justify clawing back resources, and the belief that assessment and analytics are dirty words that signal nefarious intent. Overcoming these challenges is a heavy lift.

The Intersection of Analytics and Leadership

As senior campus leaders try to use big data and the analytics revolution to benefit their colleges and universities, they need to emphasize that data are an essential resource for contending with the difficulties that their institutions face. However, research on the intersection of college and university leadership, the use of data, and the acceleration of a culture of evidence is still relatively unexplored. The Pew Research report had it right: college and university leaders will be able to articulate an ideal vision for a high-powered campus fueled by data but will struggle to execute it.[33] This book began with a desire to help senior campus leaders bridge that gap, given the evidence imperative facing colleges and universities nationwide and the untapped potential of big data and the analytics revolution to meet that demand.

The pages that follow are intended to serve as a resource to help campus leaders cultivate, implement, and sustain a culture of evidence through the adoption and use of data and analytics. Chapter 2 introduces key concepts and terms related to data and analytics and perspectives on how to set up a campus for a successful analytics journey. It also describes the analytics spectrum, which ranges from descriptive to prescriptive, to help campus leaders identify both strengths and areas where their institution could grow to facilitate the maturation of its data infrastructure and capacity. The book then focuses on how to achieve these outcomes strategically in a number of core areas. A variety of publicly available data from sources already exist, including the National Center for Educational Statistics, its Integrated Postsecondary Education Data System, and the Voluntary System of Accountability. Because the higher education community is already aware of the utility of these data sources, this book will focus instead on more recent developments in ways to use data effectively.

Defining an Aspiration

Heightened performance expectations, demands for accountability and transparency, growing social inequity, shifting demographics, concerns about cost and affordability, and an increasingly unstable financial model have converged, leaving campus leaders to wonder what the future holds. To their credit, some college presidents are intentionally converting crisis into opportunity instead of idly awaiting a reversal of fortune. One of the first steps in this process is creating a vision of a prosperous and reinvented campus that remains true to its mission, values, and identity. Data and analytics are critical for this task, especially when such goals require aggressive enrollment growth or dramatic gains in the volume and variety of degrees and certificates conferred. When it is successfully done, a well-articulated aspiration creates an initial sense of optimism and empowerment and provides an inflection point. However, once the rush subsides, questions arise. Leaders need to be ready and equipped with answers based on models that demonstrate a realistic plan forward that builds upon campus resources instead of tearing down what exists.

Focusing on Student Success and Equity

US higher education has long been regarded as a vehicle for equity and upward mobility and as foundational to our democracy. Yet equitable access and outcomes have proven to be elusive. Gaps persist at a time when a rising share of current and prospective college students come from historically marginalized or low-income backgrounds. The need to bridge these gaps has become a social and economic imperative that colleges and universities have a lead role in addressing. Many institutions are adopting analytics tools to help them do so by emphasizing enhancing the student experience both in and out of the classroom. Institutions are now gathering and making sense of a growing volume of data that identifies at-risk students so they can support them through early alert systems, proactive advising, targeted financial aid, and chatbots.

Optimizing Financial Resources

The success of a modern institution depends on its ability to effectively generate, manage, and invest resources in service of what matters most to the institution. This skill is particularly important now because the higher education financial model is in a state of flux. The increasing unreliability of traditional revenue sources, such as state funding, has prompted college leaders to reconsider how their campus approaches strategic finance. To do so successfully, senior leaders need to convince faculty and staff to use financial data in tandem with performance data so they can understand the cost and performance of their programs and services in relation to their institution's strategic direction and identity. Financial data infrastructure and the widespread use of the data are necessary for fully understanding financial costs and benefits, and few institutions are at that point. It should be noted that a well-rounded approach to strategic finance is epitomized not by across-the-board cuts or a slash-and-burn mentality. Strategic finance is not about the bottom line; it is about optimizing organizational resources. It is characterized by a balanced approach to channeling finite resources into programs and interventions that are most crucial for the sustainability and distinctiveness of colleges and universities.

Academic Renewal and Quality

The richness and relevance of academic programs weigh heavily in the decisions prospective students and their families, employers, and legislatures make about whether to attend, partner with, or support an institution. Increasingly, how an institution delivers education and services also factors into the decisions students make about which institution to attend. Today, a heightened emphasis on post-graduation outcomes, assessment and continuous improvement, and the fluidity of the transfer process and a growing reliance on contingent faculty have raised concerns that the academic core of a campus is changing in fundamental and detrimental ways. How a campus uses data and analytics to understand the expectations of students and the needs of employers and lawmakers is of the utmost importance. By doing so effectively, institutions can rebrand and align academic programs instead of starting from scratch to create new ones or disbanding others completely. Furthermore, having a robust and streamlined process for meaningful and actionable assessment can help ensure ongoing renewal of the academic core while also preserving institutional distinctiveness.

Benefits and Dangers of Analytics

The potential benefits of harnessing big data and analytics are large and well known. However, campus leaders must proceed with caution because the risks are equally great and less commonly understood. As institutions knowingly—and in some cases, unknowingly—harvest and integrate data that are increasingly sensitive and personal, efforts to adopt analytics and encourage their use at scale can become a fraught endeavor. Very quickly, mismanagement, misuse, or neglect can create perverse consequences that run counter to the strategic goals and priorities of an institution. In addition, costs can spiral out of control and infrastructure can quickly become outdated. Campus leaders need strategies that allow their institution to fully realize the value of data and analytics but also remove as many risks as possible.

Implementation and Planning

College executives stand to benefit greatly from adopting a strategic approach to the use of data and analytics, yet very few have clearly defined what such an approach looks like or, for that matter, considered how to create one. The development of a strategic approach should begin with a formal charge to use community engagement to create a clear vision. Once this aspirational state is defined, champions should be convened and given the task of taking stock of the institutional capacity to develop a culture of evidence at scale. A fully developed asset map will reveal clusters of aligned interests and complementary data, such as student success and equity. These points of intersection are ideally suited for experimentation with a codified and organized approach to data and analytics. A sound and inclusive process of implementation can help ensure a successful journey.

Colleges and universities that use data in these key areas well can help ensure the success of their students and the sustainability of their institution. College leaders have a vital role to play in realizing the full potential of data and analytics by championing an evidence-based approach that empowers the entire campus community. By focusing campus efforts and resources on the intersection of people, process, data, and technology, leaders can be the spark that ignites lasting transformational change.

Data Governance, Privacy, and Security

A frequent problem when colleges embrace data and analytics is that demands for insight eventually outstrip production capacity. This discrepancy can happen suddenly, particularly at institutions with small—but mighty—data shops that were designed for compliance and reflective analyses. Instead of waiting in line for institutional research support, stakeholders may seek shortcuts and workarounds that can be incredibly detrimental to campus-wide efforts to organize and improve the use of data. Frustration and impatience can lead to simmering tensions that contribute to communication breakdowns and inconsistent messaging. These frustrations can boil over, resulting in entrenchment, turf wars, and full-blown conflict. Over time, these disputes can erode traditional structures such as offices of institutional research, assessment, and institutional effectiveness that have long been considered gatekeepers of data and stewards of continuous improvement. Well-thought-out policies and processes, widely accessible tutorials, broadly communicated governance standards, and the use of technology can help ensure that the adoption of analytics remains focused and organized rather than chaotic.

Conclusion

When senior campus leaders work to leverage the full potential of data, numerous issues can arise that involve people, processes, data, technology, and culture. Leading a campus toward evidence-based decision-making is not an exact science. The process relies on the art of leadership, political savvy, and ability to nurture a culture that embraces the use of data as much as—if not more than—data science. College and university presidents and provosts, most of whom arrive on campus as change agents, have to win the hearts, minds, and wallets of diverse campus stakeholders who are skeptical about the benefits of effective data use. Given these challenges, creating a culture of evidence requires equal parts data-informed decision-making, logic, artful persuasion, and financial incentives. The remaining chapters of this book describe the many opportunities and challenges that colleges and universities face in their journey toward a data-enabled campus. A successful trip requires a keen understanding of current and emergent trends in data creation and analysis and a commitment to using that knowledge to increase equity and institutional sustainability.

Chapter 2

Demystifying Data and Analytics

The hype surrounding big data and advanced analytics has grown tremendously in recent years. Many senior campus leaders are eager to use big data and advanced analytics to enhance their institutions, but it can be hard to know where to start for any number of reasons, one of which is that the industry is still emerging. The terms and concepts surrounding big data and advanced analytics—infrastructure providers, data centers, analytics as service providers, networks—and the systems that capture, store, clean, integrate, analyze, and refine data are evolving at constantly accelerating rates.[1] There is also dissonance between where big data and advanced analytics are going and how colleges typically use data. Big data and advanced analytics cycle rapidly, are highly iterative, and are always on the move. Today's breakthroughs quickly become yesterday's news. However, the way colleges and universities use data has historically been siloed, static, and task specific, a configuration that is suboptimal for fully harnessing the analytics revolution.

Senior campus leaders can do two things to position themselves to take advantage of the full potential of big data and the analytics revolution. First, they can get clear about the fundamentals. Achieving a full understanding of big data and advanced analytics is a moving target and a full-time job, and college presidents, provosts, and other campus leaders have enough concerns keeping them up at night without having worry about becoming data scientists.[2] However, more and more campus leaders are making big bets on big data. As leaders organize and expand systematic approaches to the use of data and invest large amounts of time, effort, energy and money into building analytics capabilities, they need to be conversant in the key concepts and terms related to big data and advanced analytics and how they are being applied throughout higher education. Second, campus leaders can work in earnest to develop and sustain a culture of evidence, the glue that brings together the campus community and strengthens their efforts to use data.

Higher education leaders can move their institution a long way in their analytics journey by taking these two steps. This chapter offers an overview of big data and advanced analytics to facilitate a better understanding of the topic. It also provides information about the characteristics of a culture of evidence.

The Fundamentals

As they face an evidence imperative, many senior campus leaders are keen to understand how to transform the higher education business model. Given how ubiquitous big data and analytics have become in higher education, it pays to have a have a primer.

Big Data

While it is still an evolving concept, definitions of big data typically refer to the massive growth of transaction data and the explosion of new data sources, including devices such as smartphones and social media. They also frequently refer to evolving storage and archival capabilities and new technologies designed to handle these capacity issues. Big data involves multiple dimensions that initially include volume, or the amount of data; variety, the structural diversity of data; and velocity, the pace of data generation and its translation to analysis.[3] Additional dimensions have emerged more recently, such as veracity, or the accuracy and reliability of data; variability, or differences in data flow rates and the complexity and variety of data sources; and value, or the potential for data to be used to iterate, innovate, and improve.[4]

Structured and Unstructured Data

Because of the increase in varieties of data and the tools for managing and analyzing them, it is important to understand the differences between structured and unstructured data, where data resides, and how data get processed.[5] Structured data come in a predetermined format with standardized fields and storage. This model makes it easy to enter, search, and analyze data. Some common examples in higher education include data on attendance, completion rates, and grades.

Unstructured data come in different shapes and sizes. Examples include social media data, traffic data, and stock-price data. It includes images, audio, video, and qualitative data from sources that include documents (e.g., PDFs, emails, and Word files), text messages via smartphones, and social media feeds. It is estimated that roughly 95% of data today is unstructured.[6] Examples of unstructured data in higher education are student-created data, such as assignments, discussion posts, and peer assessments and reviews. While unstructured data is typically more difficult and costly to analyze, new technologies make it easier and more cost effective to do so. Because of the immense potential that lies in analyzing unstructured data, this development will be important for higher education.

Data Literacy

Data literacy, the ability to comprehend data, is an essential skill for many college and university employees. Aspects of data literacy include understanding where data come from and how they are made, techniques for analyzing data, effective interpretation of data, and clear communication of how data can be used to create value for an institution.[7] Key skills include asking the right questions, being able to choose appropriate data and test the data's validity, critical thinking, and writing. The more data literate an institution of higher education is, the better able it will be to continuously improve over time.[8]

Analytics

The Association for Institutional Research, EDUCAUSE, and the National Association of College and University Budget Officers define analytics as "the use of data, statistical analysis, and explanatory and predictive models to gain insight and act on complex issues."[9] Analytics includes the processes colleges and universities use to manage data for operational and analytical uses and analyze data using a variety of techniques. Higher education institutions use the findings from data analytics to guide institutional policy and practice, improve institutional outcomes in equitable and sustainable ways, and enhance teaching, learning, and advising.[10] Campuses use both traditional and nontraditional data sources to uncover and investigate patterns. According to the American Institutes for Research, key capabilities related to a comprehensive approach to data analytics include data collection, ensuring data quality and integration from diverse sources, and robust analysis and visualization capabilities.[11] IBM has identified a cycle of five kinds of analytics that can inform and improve decision-making: planning analytics, descriptive analytics, diagnostic analytics, predictive analytics, and prescriptive analytics.[12]

Planning Analytics

It is vitally important to define a clear purpose for any analytics plans. Planning analytics include analyzing historical performance, identifying unique patterns and trends, scenario planning, predicting outcomes, and assessing risk. Planning analytics uses data accumulated from all parts of the analytics cycle and should be continuous, active, and collaborative to ensure the delivery of timely, accurate, relevant, valid, and integrated data to promote an ongoing cycle of improvement.[13] It should conclude with a clear vision that will shape future phases of analytics, including a set of key performance indicators that establishes a common understanding of what helps or hinders campus efforts in such areas as student success and equity, academic excellence, strategic finance, and research and scholarly excellence.

Descriptive Analytics

Descriptive analytics refers to examining what has already happened. This can be a valuable process. It includes consulting the key performance indicators that were identified in the planning analytics phase and using trustworthy data that have been defined and governed properly.[14] For example, a president might ask: Did our graduation rates get better or worse? Are our students accumulating credits toward their degrees in ways that promote on-time graduation and reduce excess credits? How do these metrics vary by race, gender, income, age, and major, among other traits? A provost might inquire whether students were learning based on formative and summative assessments of student learning in courses and the quality and impact of support services. Descriptive analytics provide data that form the basis of the next step in the analytics cycle.

Diagnostic Analytics

Once descriptive analytics have been used to understand *what* happened, diagnostic analytics can be used to understand *why* something happened. During the diagnostic phase, data are generally analyzed to identify outliers. Sharp changes in student satisfaction, student performance in gatekeeper prerequisite courses, or sudden fluctuations in retention and graduation rates will prompt a deeper dive. This process of exploration can often lead to using new kinds of data or augmenting data with information collected from surveys or focus groups. More sophisticated analyses can then be used to determine whether statistically significant relationships exist, which is when advanced analytics techniques come into play.

Advanced Analytics

Advances in technology, statistical methods, and analytical techniques make it increasingly possible for the examination of data to automated using advanced analytics. According to the technological research firm Gartner, advanced analytics uses "data/text mining, machine learning, pattern matching, forecasting, visualization, semantic analysis, sentiment analysis, network and cluster analysis, multivariate statistics, graph analysis, simulation, complex event processing, neural networks" to reveal patterns that are difficult to see and make predictions and/or recommendations.[15] Three of the most well-known types of advanced analytics include predictive, prescriptive, and learning analytics.

Predictive Analytics. Predictive analytics uses regression, forecasting, predictive modeling, and multivariate statistics, among other techniques, to determine the likelihood that something will happen.[16] Defining traits of predictive analytics include an emphasis on looking ahead, rapid-cycle analyses, a focus on actionable insights that could lead to operational improvements, and ease of use and accessibility.[17]

Prescriptive Analytics. Prescriptive analytics make recommendations about what can be done to influence likely future outcomes. Common techniques include graph analysis, simulation, complex event processing, recommendation engines, and machine learning.[18]

Learning Analytics. Learning analytics is expected to reach mainstream adoption in the next few years.[19] The term refers to the collection and analysis of student data for the purpose of understanding and improving learning outcomes. Learning analytics are commonly used to identify and measure key indicators of student performance, improve student support interventions, assess the effectiveness of teaching, and inform strategic decision-making.[20] The emergence of new technologies has made the analysis of unstructured data and blended structured and unstructured data less costly and more effective. This timely development has immense potential given the rapid shift to online courses with synchronous and asynchronous dimensions during the COVID-19 pandemic.

As colleges and universities face more pressure to leverage big data and advanced analytics to promote student success, equity, and institutional sustainability, they will rely more and more on advanced analytics. Artificial intelligence will help them look around the corner and become more agile in their efforts to do so.

Artificial Intelligence (AI)

Oracle defines AI as the "systems or machines that mimic human intelligence to perform tasks and can iteratively improve themselves based on the information they collect."[21] Although recent headlines might lead one to believe that the purpose of AI is to eliminate massive numbers of jobs, AI is meant to enhance the work processes of people and organizations by streamlining redundant and onerous activities. It is generally used to deter and fend off computer security intrusions, resolve issues with technology, reduce production management through automation, and gauge internal compliance.[22] Early adopters are using AI in higher education to create chatbots to help students with frequently asked questions, predict scheduling needs based on structured and unstructured data, and develop recommendation engines that guide students through course registration.

Machine Learning

Machine learning, a subset of AI, identifies patterns in data to develop problem-solving models.[23] There are three different kinds of machine learning: supervised, unsupervised, and reinforced. Colleges and universities can use machine learning in numerous ways. For example, machine learning is already being used to identify student retention and persistence patterns and factors that influence student success, such as whether high grades in prerequisite or foundational courses affect success in a specific major. While not all AI is machine learning, all machine learning is AI.

Deep Learning Analytics and Neural Networks

Deep learning systems are a branch of AI based on the structure of the human brain. They rely on neural networks that enable computers to learn from observational data. These networks consist of thousands of layered and deeply connected processing nodes. Data items move through these network layers in one direction based on whether they reach a specific threshold.[24] Deep learning and neural networks are being used in natural language processing, facial recognition, and the creation of personalized plans in health care and education.[25]

Developing a Culture of Evidence

Despite initial enthusiasm regarding big data and the analytics revolution, colleges and universities have made only spotty progress in the effective use of these statistical tools. One of the chief reasons is a lack of a culture of evidence. A fully formed culture of evidence is present when data and analytics are used to inform decision-making broadly, consistently, and collaboratively throughout an institution. Without that culture, campuses may be at risk of misusing these tools in problematic ways (see chapter 8).

Colleges and universities that have a strong culture of evidence optimize the use of data, thus minimizing the associated risks. On a campus with a strong culture of evidence, leaders blend insights derived from analytical thinking built on quality data and methods to promote student success and equity, strategic and sustainable finance, and academic quality and integrity. This is the optimal situation, but a great deal of discord can emerge on the way to reaching the ideal state.

In reality, most colleges and universities have uneven cultures of evidence and it is not a given that a higher education institution will be data informed. Being data informed requires a level of comfort with using big data and analytics, and some organizations have reported that they feel less comfortable with analytics than they used to be.[26] Building a culture of evidence is an even bigger challenge now than it was in the past because of the rapid acceleration of data creation and analytics capabilities and the fact that colleges and universities tend to be lagging adopters. Part of the discomfort senior campus leaders feel about developing a culture of evidence is the amorphous nature of the concept and the variations in definition that exist within and across institutions.

What Is a Culture of Evidence?

According to the American Association of State Colleges and Universities' Center for Student Success,[27] a culture of evidence means making decisions based on data. Strategies are set, resources are allocated, and actions are taken based on outcomes extracted from the rigorous and continuous analysis of good data rather than on anecdotal evidence. In a culture of evidence, using data is viewed positively and new analysis is perceived as the starting point for a conversation about how to improve. Good analysis is viewed as a platform for collaboration and discussion, not as a cudgel to ensure accountability.

A culture of evidence positions a college or university to strengthen the quality of the student experience across multiple dimensions within the classroom and across the wraparound services that institutions are increasingly using to facilitate learning. It includes traditional quantitative data and so much more, such as data from focus groups, town halls, and social media. Synthesizing these various data types to identify institutional opportunities and challenges and barriers to student success is difficult but worthy work that can make a big difference if it is modeled consistently.

The American Association of State Colleges and Universities has identified the pillars that support a strong culture of evidence: leadership, governance, infrastructure and politics, established goals and accountability, and support and strategic use.[28] The reality is that traditional data from institutional research and information technology is no longer sufficient because demands have outstripped capacity. A culture of evidence helps ensure that using data is an institution-wide effort.

A culture of evidence has multiple traits that counteract the traditional ways colleges and universities use data. In a culture of evidence, data are integrated. However, campus stakeholders often have reasons for not sharing data, and that prevents colleges from understanding the intersection of scale, impact, quality, and sustainability. Moreover, without a clear statement of an institution-wide aspiration and a clearly aligned data plan and strategy, diverse college stakeholders will see the value of data differently. In a campus with a culture of evidence, the institution's strategic direction will include how it plans to blend and use data in order to overcome traditional organizational, cultural, and political silos. Clear values and purpose coupled with a positive approach to using data will work to establish trust. That task is easiest during good times and/or the honeymoon period of new leadership. Unfortunately, data is often not used in timely, accurate, relevant, and strategic ways until an imperative exists to do so. As a result, most colleges lack an understanding of the state of their analytics operations until it is too late.

Even when the stars align, college leaders may overestimate the ability of chairs, faculty, and advisors to wield data effectively. Therefore, a well-articulated rationale for using data and training for faculty and staff who do not know how to use it is important. Incentives also help, although they are difficult to provide when colleges and universities are facing economic hardship.

Jump-Starting Efforts

In order to jump-start efforts designed to build a culture of evidence, it is important to assess where a campus is versus where it wants to be regarding using data effectively. This process benefits from a framework that includes an honest assessment of leadership commitment to using data; an understanding of data governance and utility; an inventory of how data is integrated across all organizational roles, including those of faculty and advisors; understanding the degree to which the college can support the scaled-out use of evidence; and an examination of whether the institution is using data to support aspirational and operational pursuits.

If campus leaders are not invested in using data in an integrated and focused fashion, efforts to get the campus to do so may as well stop after this assessment. Presidents and provosts must articulate clearly that they are focused on student success and equity. If they do not do so, some stakeholders will continue to operate as they have in the past. This reaction is largely attributable to a desire for continuity. For example, rapid turnover within a cabinet often leads to restarts, which means that efforts to use data effectively continue to lag when they should continue even during times of transition and discontinuity. Continuity often hinges on a shared understanding of the primacy of student success throughout college efforts. Without this common purpose, diverse and disparate units and departments will march to the beat of their own drums, which means that student-focused efforts will not progress as they should. There is value in a universal and consistently applied definition of a student-focused campus.

Especially since the onset of the COVID-19 pandemic, it is vital to create equitable learning experiences for distinct student segments across diverse modalities. Many institutions have had to rapidly build out the ability to educate students remotely and asynchronously. Until these experiences and learning outcomes are equitable across time and space, colleges and universities will fail to achieve a core feature of their mission: equitable access to a quality education regardless of how students choose to engage with higher education. Broad access to equitably effective modalities is an increasingly important key to mission fulfillment and financial sustainability, and institutions that focus on it will position themselves well for the future, which looks to be decidedly focused on blended course delivery.

The blending of the educational experience extends across courses and increasingly throughout supports. Colleges and universities must therefore endeavor to restructure their organizations in such a way that students feel well informed about the different pathways to a degree or a credential. Although this restructuring can take many forms, there are some keys to success: integrating data, ensuring that metrics are universally understood, and ensuring that faculty and staff have a clear understanding of how using data to restructure the college translates to their core job duties. It is the responsibility of senior leaders and human resources personnel to include the information that job candidates are expected to use data in forward-looking ways that benefit students. Assigning these duties in a global way can eliminate the excuse that data literacy is not in someone's job description.

Successful implementation of efforts to create change requires that institutions acknowledge that acquiring an education is increasingly a journey that takes a student to multiple colleges and/or universities. Transfer policies such as articulation agreements, which were born in an era where moving from one campus to the next was far less common, work against student migration from college to college. Students are now taking increasingly unique pathways to a degree or credential, which means that standard approaches to evaluating and applying credits to general education and major requirements often mean that some a student's hard-earned credits get rejected.

Students and employers are increasingly interested in job readiness, but colleges remain apprehensive about or incapable of helping students understand the value of graduating and have not yet effectively used employment and earnings data to their full potential to prepare students for careers. This disconnect is unfortunate and has led to a growing sentiment among employers that colleges and universities are doing a poor job of preparing their students for work. This is partly attributable to a reluctance among faculty and advisors to translate the contents of an academic transcript to discreet skills and competencies that students can communicate easily and employers can understand. Career advising should be a fundamental part of preparing students to effectively translate their hard-earned skills into a value proposition that employers understand. Given that a growing number of colleges find themselves serving low-income, first-generation, and underrepresented students who lack career networks and professional role models, data related to postgraduate outcomes should be welcomed into the classroom, not cast aside.

Tying It All Together

A deeper understanding of the full universe of data and methods of analysis coupled with an awareness of the changing nature of student needs and expectations can position a college to use data well. Leaders must be on board with the project of proactively building a culture of evidence that institutionalizes effective use of data, clearly articulates institutional aspirations and values, focuses on equity (both in traditional terms and across modalities), prioritizes student-centered pathways, and integrates postgraduate data for the purposes of advising students and maximizing the value of their education. Once this vision is articulated, a college can begin to take steps toward realizing it. A culture of evidence and effective use of data includes relevant data that are accurate and available to the right people at the right time; specific metrics that are measurable, achievable, and timebound; a focus on assessment of student learning and continuous improvement; routine use of mechanisms that monitor and track progress; patience; and incentives.

Conclusion

The emergence of big data and advanced analytics presents a clear opportunity for a paradigm shift regarding how colleges and universities use data. As Randy L. Swing has noted, this shift has been under way for some time.[29] Recent changes to the higher education environment will likely accelerate the adoption of big data and advanced analytics. These environmental changes began nearly two decades ago when the Organisation for Economic Co-Operation and Development (OECD) revealed that the rate of postsecondary degree attainment in the United States had slipped below the top ten rates among OECD countries.[30] This news led federal and state legislatures to mobilize to improve degree attainment. This effort, known as the completion agenda, included greater demands for accountability and performance data. As a result, major equity gaps were brought to national attention.

So began a massive shift among colleges and universities from being teaching centered toward being learner centered, equity driven, and data informed. The immense disruptions caused by the COVID-19 pandemic and the economic crash, political tensions, and calls for social justice since 2020 will likely speed up and solidify the need for colleges and universities to use big data and advanced analytics in diverse and increasingly sophisticated ways. However, they are but tools to be used effectively and ethically. A culture of evidence must also be developed, which requires a commitment from leaders; a clear focus; empowerment of faculty and staff; a well-designed framework for governance, utility, and engagement; and infrastructure and policies that allow for the widespread and effective adoption of big data and advances analytics.

A clear understanding of the key concepts and trends related to the creation, evolution, integration, and analysis of data are prerequisites for building a college or university that is well equipped and enthusiastic about using data and advanced analytical tools. Leadership of all types within a campus—from presidents and provosts to cabinet members, deans, department chairs, all the way down to individual advisors—can unlock the capacity of data and analytics. Success is often predicated on the capacity of campus leaders to align aspirational goals and strategies with more granular school and departmental goals. These goals often focus on student success and equity, strategic finance, and academic quality and integrity. A focus on issues related to data governance, privacy, and security will help ensure that efforts driven by data analysis reduce barriers to student success, such as implicit bias within data, analyses, and people. One of the most important first steps toward convincing a college to embrace using data is defining an aspiration that embodies the uniqueness of the institution and paints a picture of a future that honors its rich mission, vision, and values.

Chapter 3

Defining an Institutional Aspiration Using Data

One of the defining traits of US higher education is its diversity. Each campus has unique features that can make it stand out among its peers if they are properly understood and effectively communicated. As the traditionally aged college-going population plateaus and declines in some regions of the country, state budgets tighten up, and the knowledge and learning economy grows, competition among campuses will intensify. Institutions that do not stand out because of their unique characteristics and offerings will feel these changes particularly keenly. Unfortunately, the status hierarchy in higher education is set up to incentivize colleges and universities to follow the herd and conform to the notion that they should be all things to all people. As a result, one of the perverse consequences of pursuing rankings and prestige is that on the surface, higher education looks increasingly homogenous to prospective students, would-be funders, government agencies, and watchdogs. This trend provides stakeholders with a reason to look beyond a generic campus toward other, more distinct institutions, but it also provides ammunition for those eager to find reasons to slash, cut, consolidate, or close programs or campuses, often with little precision or nuance. It is therefore incumbent upon presidents and senior campus leaders to take a hard, deep look at their institutions using qualitative and quantitative data.

Sources for Redefining Institutional Aspirations

A number of common truths relate to setting ambitious agendas on higher education campuses. First, *it is rare for an institution to truly abandon its founding purpose or original context.* Given that tradition, any ambitious agenda or modernization effort should refer to an institution's guiding principles whenever possible. For example, Cornell University's motto, "I would found an institution where any person can find instruction in any study," was first penned by Ezra Cornell in a letter to the university's first president.[1] Cornell University is both an Ivy League institution and New York state's federal land-grant institution, and it has unique partnership schools in the State University of New York system. These arrangements are admittedly rare and sit at the intersection of a wide variety of academic disciplines, a commitment to education for the public good, and a desire to foster inclusivity. In 2019, the Cornell campus community reimagined the core values from in a motto more than 150 years old to reflect contemporary challenges and opportunities.[2] A future state based on the founding principles of the college is a much easier sell.

Second, *it is important to build on existing goals and strategies, so look around and ask questions.* People have worked hard on strategy and planning, often endlessly and without recognition. They understandably get frustrated when that work is overlooked, intentionally or not. Leaders should carefully review, synthesize, and point to the key themes and symmetries that exist between previous and current self-evaluation and planning efforts, emphasizing the importance of defining a new aspirational strategy.

Accreditation Documents

A campus-wide self-study, particularly if it was recent or is on-going, is an ideal vehicle for considering and unpacking a campus's strengths and opportunities for improvement. By virtue of the process, the conclusion of an accreditation cycle has a way of resurfacing and harmonizing a college's core values and beliefs. It reveals data trends in key areas, such as assessment of student learning outcomes, that under normal circumstances would be more difficult to obtain. Successful self-studies generate a sense of pride and optimism among campus constituents and lay the groundwork for future planning. The last few institutional self-studies should provide a comprehensive history of the campus that spans decades. This content is incredibly valuable and leaders should immerse themselves in it.

Documentation of Recent Strategic Plans and Guiding Statements

The concept that much remains consistent even as change happens certainly applies to the strategic plans and mission, vision, and values statements of colleges and universities. If twenty college strategic plans were randomly chosen for review, common themes would emerge, such as some form of equitable access and student success; academic quality and excellence; research, scholarly, and creative activity; economic development and stewardship of place; and strategic finance and campus sustainability. These themes would be contextualized, of course, to account for an institution's academic curriculum, areas of research focus, student population, local and regional demands, and areas of excellence and pride. Another issue is that campus strategic plans tend to last too long, running five or more years in most cases. As a result, many need to be refreshed, which is an ideal opportunity to think ambitiously and set new goals.

Campus mission and vision statements run the gamut from streamlined to verbose, but they rarely deviate substantially from previous iterations. Word count plus how much or how little a text has evolved over time can reveal important hints about the culture of the campus that will either help or hinder efforts to define an aspiration.

Governance Documents and Senate Minutes

The records of campus governance structures, such as the college or academic senate and its subcommittees, often contain hot-button topics that reveal murky areas that lie between administrative and academic prerogatives. These gray areas can be hidden landmines, but if they are properly leveraged, they can be opportunities for collaboration. Awareness of these issues and thoughtful engagement with them during the process of defining institutional aspirations can position the effort for success.

Legislative Mandates

Sometimes external stakeholders can help jump-start efforts to define an aspiration. For example, in 1997, the Kentucky General Assembly passed higher education reforms in the Postsecondary Education Improvement Act of 1997, which is known within the commonwealth as House Bill 1.[3] The act created the Council on Postsecondary Education, the statewide higher education coordinating body, as a first step toward creating a seamless, integrated postsecondary system. The plan purposefully included strategic areas that were tailored to help each college and university, regardless of type, have an opportunity to excel. House Bill 1 provided a framework that each campus has continued to use to shape short-term and long-term strategies and represents a consensus-driven approach to a statewide aspiration at its best.

Goals of the System or Coordinating Board

In recent years, the higher education governing or coordinating bodies of many states have passed bold educational attainment goals. A large number have also moved toward some form of performance funding models. For example, the Texas Higher Education Coordinating Board launched the 60x30TX Plan in 2015.[4] It calls for 60% of the 25- to 34-year-old population of Texas to hold a certificate or degree by 2030. At the time the plan was launched, 35% of Texans held an associate degree or higher and there were concerns that the rate would decline based on demographic shifts within the state. Similarly, in 2015, the California State University system launched Graduation Initiative 2025, which was developed to significantly increase graduation rates among first-time and transfer students.[5] Graduation Initiative 2025 built upon the first Graduation Initiative, which began in 2009. Building on past initiatives can be good strategy, and goals set by governance structures can provide part of the rationale for campus- or system-level reforms.

Listening Tours

Listening and hearing are important when embarking on an effort to define a new aspiration for a college or university. Campus town halls, focus groups, and platforms for input often address cross-cutting themes that can help a leader align the various agendas of faculty, students, and staff. They also represent a rich source of qualitative data and a record that memorializes how the campus community currently sees itself—and what it aspires to be.

A deep understanding of the campus's uniqueness can be informed by the history of strategic planning efforts, topics of discussion that frequently arise, points of intersection between administrators and academics, the nature of system and legislative goals and strategies, and campus-wide conversations. Data from these sources can converge to form the foundation upon which an aspiration can be built and sustained. Once that foundation becomes visible, senior campus leaders can begin to use data to build a vision of a future state that honors the identity of the campus.

Advice for Campus Leaders

Be Willing to Be Uncomfortable with First Reponses to a New Vision

It is no secret that many campuses are data rich and information poor. Many institutional research offices lack the capacity to move beyond fulfilling ad hoc requests for information and producing compliance reports, even if the desire to do more exists. As a result, creating predictive machine learning models that sift through the entire universe of campus data is a pipe dream for many institutions. However, that deficit should not deter a college or university from designing an aspirational future state. In fact, sometimes institutions can overcomplicate matters when it comes to creating big and audacious goals. Focusing on the historical performance data of a campus that has operated rather steadily for many years is unlikely to inspire new goals that look and feel appreciably different.

While the process of defining an aspiration should be somewhat familiar, it should also cause productive discomfort. The introduction of relatively static—or in some cases stagnant—data can quickly kill the mood for thinking big, but this response should not be taken as resistance or entrenchment. In fact, it is the sign that a campus is behaving as it should. Long-tenured deans, distinguished professors, and department chairs who have been at the institution for decades and directors and other management professionals all represent the sustaining leadership that most colleges and universities nationwide enjoy. As it is the job of these stakeholders to make sure that the institution functions on a daily basis without straying too far from its roots, presidents and senior leadership teams should expect them to challenge leaders when they broach the idea of a bold aspiration. Skepticism should be considered a good thing, so long as it is healthy. A compelling and plausible case for change is needed, and it is the role of the president, supported by senior campus leadership and governance, to be persuasive when they present a new vision.

Keep It High Level and Estimate Internal Impact

Drawing on currently available data to demonstrate what progress will look like if current trends continue is a good place to start the discussion about defining institutional aspirations. Senior leaders can start by examining recent graduation rates and numbers of degrees conferred. If national trends are any indication of the performance of the school, it will likely have seen a gradual uptick in graduation rates and degrees conferred. According to the National Center for Educational Statistics, the six-year graduation rate for first-year students who entered four-year postsecondary institutions in 2012 (62.4%) was 7 percentage points higher than that of the first-year students who entered in 1996 (55.4%).[6] At two-year institutions, the three-year graduation rate increased just over 2 percentage points when comparing first-year students who entered in 2000 (30.5%) and first-year students who entered in 2015 (32.6%).[7] To some, gradual progress is acceptable, especially when put in the context some of the major challenges facing higher education today. Still, focusing on outcomes with disregard for equity is shortsighted. Colleges must align what they do with the emerging majority within the student body.

Any doubt about accelerating progress can be overcome if senior leaders can help campus stakeholders understand that plenty of opportunities for improvement exist without strapping dynamite to the foundations of the campus. Take for example, a public four-year campus whose six-year graduation rates—an imperfect measure of success to be sure—has increased from 40% to 50% over the course of a decade. This accomplishment is impressive, and the campus community might think replicating it an impossible task. However, more inclusive measures such as the Student Achievement Measures and National Student Clearinghouse have emerged in recent years. These sources could help demonstrate that increasing graduation rates by another 10 percentage points is not only possible but perhaps even imminently achievable by showing in timely ways that a large percentage of students leave one campus and graduate from other institutions (figure 3.1). As a result of reviewing more contemporary standards, a college's president and senior campus leadership might come to the logical conclusion that the institution had not yet reached its ceiling. Indeed, the six-year graduation rate could be as much as 13% higher, the four-year transfer graduation rate could be bumped up a few percentage points, and a higher percentage of part-time transfer students could earn a degree.

In the example in figure 3.1, up to 198 more students would earn a degree from the institution: ninety-one more first-time degree-seeking students, thirty-two full-time transfer students, and seventy-five part-time transfer students. One year of continued study by these students would also positively affect revenues.

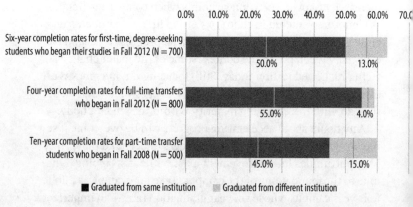

Figure 3.1. Using data to determine actual versus possible graduation rates

Colleges are naturally competitive places that want their students to succeed. In addition, few would turn their backs on helping more students earn a degree while contributing to the campus's bottom line. Analyses similar to the hypothetical example in figure 3.1 can focus on the total number of degrees earned or enrollment or student success. Regardless of the variable under consideration, the data certainly should be viewed through the lens of equity.

Focus on Equity

It is vitally important to define an aspirational strategy through the lens of equity and social justice. A focus on equity is especially needed given the continued gaps in access and outcomes and the recent social unrest that has highlighted inequities and injustice. So in addition to demonstrating who goes elsewhere to graduate, it is important to show who is more or less likely to graduate from the campus. If the college in the hypothetical example above took a deeper dive into its graduation rates, it might discover a great deal of inequity in outcomes.

In addition to race and ethnicity, colleges and universities should look at gaps based on the intersectionality of race and gender. They should also review differential outcomes based on income levels, age, enrollment intensity, and other factors.[8] When campus communities discover data that suggest an equity issue, it generally inspires a moment of self-reflection because equity gaps point to structural problems within a college or university—and within society. Equity gaps are not indications that a particular student demographic is somehow deficient or less able to succeed. Colleges want to be a part of the solution and are likely to see inequities as a call to make significant change that will address systemic obstacles. Equity has been more purposefully interwoven into the aspirations and goals of colleges and universities in recent years, as it should be.

Estimate Impact and Create a Value Proposition

The difficult process of taking stock of institutional strengths and opportunities for improvement, distilling and reaffirming enduring themes and timeless features of the institution, and studying institutional data is worthwhile because it builds trust, strengthens relationships, and gives members of the campus community confidence in their ability to rise to an aspirational challenge. The next step in defining an aspiration is developing an impact estimate and value proposition that resonates with both the internal campus community and communities beyond the institution. Well-crafted value propositions often focus on people, communities, and economies. Specific tools can help a campus in this process, and for most students and families, employers, and legislatures, a good place to start is return on investment. This return often means jobs and earnings.

The messages conveyed to prospective students and families must be appropriate, especially given the devastating economic impact of the COVID-19 pandemic. The idea of investing in a college education is increasingly scary now that job prospects are lower than they have been in eighty years. People want to know whether investing in a college education will be worth it. Numerous data sources can help a college answer with a resounding "Yes!" As was the case with the Great Recession of 2008–2009, the aftermath of the pandemic has hit individuals with the lowest levels of educational attainment the hardest (table 3.1).[9]

A college education is still the best insulation against a traumatic economic downturn. United States Census Bureau data documents that earning a college degree can net more than a million dollars in earnings over a lifetime, which is twice as much as a high school graduate is projected to earn.[10] This trend applies broadly to the higher education sector, so there is little point in differentiating one institution type from another, especially public and private not-for-profit institutions. It is better to not compare

TABLE 3.1. *Graduation rate and equity gaps by race, ethnicity, and enrollment type, select years (hypothetical example)*

Race/ethnicity	First-time full-time degree-seeking students		Full-time transfers		Part-time transfers	
	2012–2018	Equity gap	2015–2018	Equity gap	2008–2018	Equity gap
Black	44	11	46	10	43	4
Latinx	47	8	48	8	44	3
American Indian/Alaskan Native	50	5	52	4	34	13
Native Hawaiian/Other Pacific Islander	40	15	38	18	40	7
Two or more races	42	13	40	16	40	7
Asian	52	3	54	2	47	0
White	55	0	56	0	47	0
Overall	50	—	55	—	45	—

Note: Equity gaps are percentage point differences between the graduation rate of a specific race/ethnicity and the graduation rate of white students.

one institution's impact estimates with those of other campuses. Instead, college leaders should seek out unique value propositions based on the identity of their campus and the community their institution serves (table 3.2).

Using Census Bureau data, college leaders can quickly determine whether their community is historically underserved. If that is the case, acquiring a college education becomes a moral and economic imperative. The hypothetical data in table 3.3 shows that the college serves a large portion of a state population that is younger and diverse, is less educated, and has a significant proportion of poor residents. Whereas some campus leaders might see such data as a huge challenge, the reality is that serving a population with low levels of educational attainment is an opportunity to demonstrate disproportionate positive impact. The education the institution provides in this hypothetical example would warrant attention and support because it relates to equity and upward mobility.

With advances in the use of data, the emergence of state longitudinal data systems, and innovative partnerships between higher education systems such as the University of Texas System and the Census Bureau, postgraduate outcomes data have become easier to access and analyze. New tools, such as SeekUT, combine data on earnings from unemployment insurance wage records, college outcomes from the National Student Clearinghouse, and data from the Census and Bureau of Labor Statistics to provide a more comprehensive picture of postgraduate outcomes that resonate with students and their families and external stakeholders including private employers and legislators.[11] These outcomes data are more compelling to use than the types of data in the tables. A campus can deeply analyze reams of data to unpack the value of the education it provides in such areas as earnings, civic engagement, and public health. However, if used properly, the combination of internal data that can be found in a campus's factbook and widely available external quality data, including data from federal sources such as the United States Census Bureau and

TABLE 3.2. *Unemployment rate among the US civilian population age 25 years and older by educational attainment, January–May 2020*

Educational attainment	Seasonally adjusted unemployment rate				
	January	February	March	April	May
Less than high school diploma	5.50	5.70	6.80	21.20	19.90
High school graduates, no college	3.80	3.60	4.40	17.30	15.30
Some college or associate degree	2.80	3.00	3.70	15.00	13.30
Bachelor's degree and higher	2.00	1.90	2.50	8.40	7.40

Source: U.S. Bureau of Labor Statistics, "Table A-4: Employment Status of the Civilian Population 25 Years and Over by Educational Attainment," June 5, 2020, https://www.bls.gov/news.release/empsit.to4.htm.

TABLE 3.3. *Important community statistics that college and university leaders should know (hypothetical data)*

Data category	State	Region	Community
Population estimates	5,000,000	2,000,000	1,000,000
Persons under age 18 years	22.00%	24.00%	30.00%
Persons age 65+ years	17.00%	14.00%	12.00%
Black or African American	18.00%	25.00%	45.00%
American Indian/Alaska Native	3.00%	2.00%	2.00%
Asian alone	9.00%	14.00%	5.00%
Native Hawaiian/Other Pacific Islander	0.10%	0.20%	0.30%
Two or more races	2.60%	3.30%	3.70%
Latinx	10.00%	30.00%	60.00%
White alone, not Latinx	60.00%	30.00%	10.00%
Households with a computer	90.00%	85.00%	80.00%
Households with a broadband Internet subscription	80.00%	75.00%	70.00%
High school graduate or higher, persons aged 25 years or more	88.00%	80.00%	70.00%
Bachelor's degree or higher, persons aged 25 years or more	37.00%	33.00%	18.00%
Median household income	$65,000	$60,000	$36,000
Per capita income in past 12 months	$38,000	$37,000	$18,000
Persons living in poverty	14.00%	20.00%	30.00%

the Integrated Postsecondary Education Data System (IPEDS), are enough to create an aspiration that tells the story of a campus on the move.

Case Study: Lehman College

In 2017, José Luis Cruz had just been named the third president in the 50-year history of Lehman College. He saw a campus with a rich history and legacy that was poised to make a major difference in its community. The Bronx, one of poorest and most inequitable counties in the nation, had one of the lowest levels of educational attainment.[12] Being born in the Bronx increases a person's likelihood of living in poverty and going to jail and decreases the chances that a person will earn a living wage. These issues are not just attributable to government neglect. Rather, the long odds Bronxites face stem from decades, if not centuries, of systematic marginalization and oppression of its residents. Census Bureau data for 2021 showed that the borough population was 56% Latinx and 44% Black or African American. Only 20.1% of the population had attained a bachelor's degree or higher.[13]

Located on a beautiful 37-acre tree-lined campus named for a governor and state senator known for his commitment to social justice and a global perspective, Lehman College is considered one of the crown jewels of the Bronx. The college was preparing to celebrate its fiftieth anniversary and had just launched its accreditation self-study, which it was planning to use as a springboard for its upcoming strategic planning process and, more important, for the campus's next fifty years. It was against this backdrop that President Cruz began the process of getting to know the campus and its community. What surfaced through his efforts was a compelling aspirational goal to substantially grow Lehman's impact on the Bronx that was called the 90 x 30 Challenge. The college sought to award 90,000 or more degrees from the beginning of the initiative through 2030, roughly double of what the college would have awarded based on analysis of historical data.[14]

The goal focused on creating prosperity and equity with an emphasis on the Bronx and the greater New York City region. Using data from the Census Bureau and the College Board's Trends in College Pricing, Lehman College created a remarkable value proposition: the impact that 45,000 high-quality credentials would have on the Bronx and the state would include nearly $7 billion in additional income, roughly $3 billion in tax revenues, and tens of thousands of people lifted out of poverty. The aspiration was designed with equity in mind, based on the reality that 93% of the college's students were people of color, 55% of students were Latinx, and 59% of undergraduates came from households with an income of $30,000 or less. In the process of focusing on enriching the lives of the people of the Bronx, Lehman College recommitted to its identity as a liberal arts institution and its history as an engine of upward mobility and social justice. Lehman College was modernizing while remaining true to itself.

The 90 x 30 Challenge was launched after nearly a year of studying the feasibility of such a grand aspiration. Numerous models based on data like those previously mentioned in this chapter were introduced to faculty, students, and staff in an effort to generate a clear aspiration for the future of the college. While in some ways the 90 x 30 Challenge marked a new beginning for Lehman College, it honored and built on the hard work and dedication of the preceding five decades. In the ensuing years, the college has seen a massive jump in enrollment and significant gains in graduation and retention rates. The American Council on Education and the Equality of Opportunity Project have recognized the college as one of the top vehicles of upward mobility among Hispanic-serving institutions.[15]

The biggest sign that the 90 x 30 Challenge stands out as a national model for aspirational strategies is that it endured even after even after a presidential transition. The importance of student success, equity, and upward mobility cannot be overstated. Too few institutions of higher education focus on their distinctive value proposition. Resilient students use the degrees they earn to create greater opportunity and more prosperous and sustainable lives. At a time when structures seem to work against this noble pursuit, colleges and universities stand out for their commitment to advancing it for people from all walks of life.

Chapter 4

Equity and Student Success

In the United States, oppression and social injustice have long been a part of life for people of color, immigrants, and the poor. For many privileged members of our society, this reality has come into focus only in recent years as protests against police brutality, systemic racism, and wealth inequality have come to characterize modern progressive movements. Demands for changes to the ways society treats specific populations have grown more widespread, leading people to seek ways to reassemble major social institutions to promote rather than hinder a more just and equitable society. Colleges and universities are among the institutions being called upon to reconsider their role.

Ensuring equitable access to higher education and achieving outcomes that contribute to upward mobility for underserved groups has proven to be an elusive goal.[1] Gaps persist at a time when an increasing share of current and prospective college students comes from historically marginalized populations or low-income families. Bridging these gaps has become a social and economic imperative that colleges and universities are uniquely poised to address. Many institutions are using data in innovative ways to help them enhance the student experience both inside and outside the classroom. By gathering and making sense of a growing volume of data, institutions are now identifying students who may benefit from proactive outreach and the development and use of tools such as early alert systems, proactive advising, targeted financial aid, and chatbots. This chapter details how a college or university can leverage data and analytics to spring into action and follow through on its stated goals and values regarding equitable access to higher education.

Growing Awareness of the Importance of Analytics

The attitude of higher education leaders about the use of data and analytics to increase student success and equity has been surprisingly harmonious in recent years. The *American College President Study 2017* points to the growing importance of data-informed decision-making related to student success.[2] In the survey for that study, college and university presidents identified retention rates, graduation rates, and minority student outcomes as the most legitimate metrics of institutional performance. Moreover, 90% of campuses have a primary data goal of improving student outcomes through interventions.[3]

The 2019 joint statement on analytics by the Association for Institutional Research, EDUCAUSE, and the National Association of College and University Business Officers underscored the importance of using data to serve students better: "We strongly believe that using data to better understand our students and our own operations paves the way to developing new, innovative approaches for improved student recruiting, better student outcomes, greater institutional efficiency and cost-containment, and much more."[4] Colleges and universities recognize the importance of effectively serving increasingly diverse students with different college-going patterns and needs, even if doing so has been a challenge in the past. The reality is that these students are the future and they need to be served well, even if that requires institutional change. Data and analytics are tools that can strengthen these efforts.

Different Times, Different Students, Different Needs

Recent research shows that the modern college-going student is not the recent high school graduate entering a residential four-year campus that many people picture when they think about who goes to college. Nearly three-quarters of US students today have at least one post-traditional characteristic.[5] A 2017 study conducted by the Office of Educational Technology of the U.S. Department of Education found that 66% of all undergraduate students transferred between institutions before they graduated, 63% were first-generation students, 62% worked full- or part-time, 43% attended part-time, and 28% had at least one dependent.[6] Louis Soares, Jonathan Gagliardi, and Christopher Nellum have noted that nearly 58% of all 2011-12 undergraduate students were post-traditional learners over the age of 25 who worked full-time, were financially independent, and/or were connected with the military and that post-traditional learners were disproportionately women and people of color.[7]

Post-traditional undergraduates are likely to constitute a significant proportion of student bodies in future years for a few reasons. Demographic projections indicate that there will be fewer high school graduates for the foreseeable future and that those who do graduate will come from increasingly diverse backgrounds. The National Center for Education Statistics projects that in 2027, nearly four in ten students enrolled at a college or university will be age 25 or older—a slightly higher rate than today, as table 4.1 notes.[8]

Modern students need a more fluid higher education ecosystem that helps them prioritize and accommodate competing life priorities, such as work or caregiving. They need academic programs and curriculum that are more reflective of their diverse backgrounds and perspectives. Additionally, the need for lifelong

TABLE 4.1. *Total projected enrollment in US degree-granting postsecondary institutions by age, 2020 and 2027 (in thousands)*

Age category	2020		2027	
	N	Percent	N	Percent
24 years old and under	12,276	61.24	12,387	60.56
25 years old and over	7,771	38.76	8,066	39.44
Total	20,047	100.00	20,453	100.00

Source: Thomas D. Snyder, Cristobal de Brey, and Sally A. Dillow, *Digest of Education Statistics*, 53rd ed. (Washington, DC: U.S. Department of Education, last modified January 2019), 409, table 303.40, https://nces.ed.gov/pubs2018/2018070.pdf.

learning and the ever-growing importance of adult and continuing education will lead to a growing number of ways to access higher education, including short-cycle credentials, digital badges, asynchronous programs, and more intentional alumni engagement. Innovations also include credit for prior learning, which has been shown to boost adult student completion rates by as much as 17% and save students between $1,500 and $10,200 and up to fourteen months of time toward earning their degrees.[9]

The successful institution of the future will adapt to accommodate contemporary students. The singular higher education business model will be supplanted by a plurality of models that include but are not restricted to the traditional on-campus experience. A more nuanced approach will be required in order to deliver high-quality academic and student experiences that come in forms as diverse as the students who are being served. The higher education community is a long way away from fulfilling these needs well, however. Look no further than persistent and troubling equity gaps for evidence.

In the period 1997–2017, the US population changed substantially. These changes were characterized by two primary trends: the white population shrank substantially as a proportion of the nation's population while the Latinx population grew (table 4.2).

TABLE 4.2. *US population by race and ethnicity, 1997, 2003, 2017 (by percent)*

Race/ethnicity	1997[a]	2003	2017
American Indian/Alaska Native	0.8	0.6	0.7
Asian	3.7	4.0	5.7
Black	12.5	12.1	12.3
Latinx	11.1	13.8	18.0
Native Hawaiian/Other Pacific Islander	—	0.2[b]	0.3
White	71.9	68.0	61.0
More than one race	—	1.4	1.9

Source: Lorelle L. Espinosa, Jonathan M. Turk, Morgan Taylor, and Hollie M. Chessman, *Race and Ethnicity in Higher Education: A Status Report* (Washington, DC: American Council on Education, 2019), table 1.2.

[a] In 1997, the only racial demographic categories reported were Hispanic, White, Black, American Indian, Eskimo, or Aleut, and Asian or Pacific Islander.
[b] The report attached a note to this cell: "Interpret with caution. Ratio of standard error is >50%."

Even in 2020, higher education equity was uneven in terms of access, persistence, and completion measures. According to the 2020 *Indicators of Higher Education Equity* report:[10]

- College participation rates vary greatly by income. The gap in college enrollment between dependent students 18 to 24 years old in the highest and lowest income quartiles was 24 percentage points in 2018, although this divide has decreased from 43 percentage points in 1990 and 46 percentage points in 1970.[11]
- Participation in college varies greatly by race and ethnicity. College participation rates among students 18 to 24 years old in 2018 were 7 percentage points higher for white students (64%) than for Black and Latinx students (57%). These gaps have only changed slightly since 1976.[12]
- Undergraduate students are increasingly diverse. From 2000 to 2016, the proportion of students of color increased from 36% to 49% for independent students and from 29% to 46%

for dependent students. Independent students are also more likely than dependent students to have completion risk characteristics.[13]

- Bachelor's degree attainment is highly inequitable by income. In 2018, a student from the highest income quartile was 3.9 times (62%) more likely to earn a bachelor's degree by age 24 than a student from the lowest income quartile (16%). Additionally, family income gaps among dependent students have risen over time.[14]
- Black and Latinx students are earning a larger proportion of degrees than in the past, but not large enough. Black and Latinx students remain underrepresented among degree earners relative to their representation in the nation's population.

Although the country has rapidly become more diverse, outcomes have lagged. This discrepancy is important because data from the National Center for Education Statistics indicates that students now enrolled in public elementary and secondary schools are now majority-minority and that the entire US population will be majority-minority within the next thirty years.[15] Equity gaps need to be closed quickly.

Consumers of Higher Education Data

Colleges and universities have many reasons to focus on equity and student success. In recent years, campuses around the country have struggled to balance academic freedom and free speech rights as incidents of hate speech have increased.[16] Insensitivity and inaction related to these issues led to the resignation of the president of the University of Missouri system and the chancellor of the University of Missouri's Columbia campus.[17] Presidents and senior campus leaders are looking for ways to communicate their institutional commitment to equitable access and outcomes.[18] One of the best ways they can do so is through actions that lead to demonstrable improvements for low-income students and students of color.

As the student population continues to diversify and pressures to solve the nation's equity problems loom large, colleges and universities are looking to address these challenges by using data in more targeted and nuanced ways. This process begins not by isolating equity as a stand-alone institutional goal but by ensuring that it is foundational to and prominently featured in all goals. This approach ensures that whatever measurement framework a campus uses includes equity metrics and is contextualized to the unique traits of a college, including but not limited to mission, student population, institutional learning outcomes, and academic programs.

Laura Fingerson and David Troutman note that measurement frameworks are shaped by external and internal stakeholders.[19] External stakeholders (e.g., a state legislature, think tanks, prospective students) are often interested in aggregate data related to student success. Internal stakeholders (e.g., department chairs, faculty, advisors) typically want to see data disaggregated at the program or service level in the form of counts (e.g., number of degrees awarded), derived variables (e.g., graduation rates), or generated data (e.g., a likelihood-of-success metric created by predictive analysis).[20]

Alicia Dowd and her colleagues have suggested that these measures need to be disaggregated by individual student characteristics (e.g., race/ethnicity, gender, age, enrollment intensity, Pell grant status), or, as they termed it, "the actionable N."[21] By looking at the intersectionality of these traits, for example by disaggregating a graduation rate by race/ethnicity and gender, internal stakeholders can act on data to promote equity.[22] When paired with measurement frameworks that integrate student success, performance, and cost data, institutions can accelerate their efforts to become a more equitable and sustainable college. Recently, the Institute for Higher Education Policy developed such a framework (table 4.3).[23]

TABLE 4.3. Institute for Higher Education Policy's Postsecondary Metrics Framework

Metric category	Access	Measures	Completion	Cost	Post-college outcomes
Performance	Enrollment	Credit accumulation Other course completion Gateway course completion Program of study selection Retention Persistence	Graduation Transfer out Success Completers	Net price Unmet need Cumulative debt	Earnings Employment Loan repayment Graduate education Learning outcomes
Efficiency	Expenditures per student	Cost of uncompleted credits Gateway completion costs Change in revenue from change in retention	Time to credential Credits to credential Cost of excess credits Completions per student	Student share of cost Expenditures per completion	Earnings threshold
Equity	Enrollment by at least the following metrics: Preparation Income Age Race/ethnicity	Progression performance by at least the following metrics: Preparation Income Age Race/ethnicity	Completion performance and efficiency by at least the following metrics: Preparation Income Age Race/ethnicity	Net price Unmet need Debt by at least the following metrics: Income Age Race/ethnicity Completion status	Outcomes performance and efficiency by at least the following metrics: Income Age Race/ethnicity Completion status

Source: IHEP, "Who Collects Which Postsecondary Data?" n.d., https://www.ihep.org/wp-content/uploads/2017/04/uploads_docs_pubs_ihep_toward_convergence_appendix_crosswalk.pdf.

The adoption of these frameworks allows colleges and universities to tailor their use of data for a number of potential audiences, including:

- State legislators who are keen to ensure that public funds are being well spent.
- Campus leaders who need a high-level view of patterns and trends related to student success and equity.
- Department chairs and individual faculty members who engage in the rigorous processes of academic planning and continuous improvement.
- Registrars and business officers who try to make the most of limited campus space and resources.
- Enrollment management and student affairs officers concerned with enhancing the experiences of students throughout the entire life cycle.
- Advancement officers who are tasked with seeking opportunities for external financial support.
- Librarians who are increasingly focused on providing open educational resources in order to maintain an affordable education.
- Students who can use this information to inform how they plan their academic journey.

Standardized data reports can be automated so that current data are delivered routinely to diverse campus stakeholders. Once a solid measurement framework has been implemented and embraced, the campus can conduct ad hoc analyses of campus structures and policies that create barriers to student success and equity. These kinds of studies often feature qualitative data, which are especially useful for getting at the reasons why something happened. Qualitative data are especially good at capturing the student perspective. Recently, a move beyond surveys to include focus groups has helped colleges make real-time decisions about how to deliver critical programs and resources.

Using Data and Analytics to Act

In the last decade, concerns over equitable access to postsecondary education have been supplanted by a desire for equitable outcomes. As a result, policymakers and vendors have collaborated with institutions to develop data and analytics capabilities of many varieties. While some colleges have taken full advantage of advanced capabilities such as artificial intelligence and machine learning, many more have adopted more rudimentary capabilities with positive results. Despite the headlines surrounding cases of more advanced use of analytics, most campuses still stand to benefit from adopting a set of staple analyses that can be done without a sophisticated algorithm, expensive software, or memberships in external analytics services.

One of the first things a college can do is to identify specific barriers to student success. In 2019, the Education Advisory Board identified 116 leading indicators that can help campuses identify barriers to equity.[24] These barriers span the entire student life cycle and cover areas that include pre-college academic preparation, student expectations and student self-efficacy, financial considerations, campus climate, pedagogy and the academic experience, college navigation, policies and procedures, and post-graduate outcomes.

Once indicators are identified, an institution can begin the process of analyzing them. The Education Trust profiled several high-performing and fast-gaining institutions in 2013.[25] A sample from that data is included in table 4.4.

Demands are growing for colleges and universities to provide equitable access to an affordable education of value and to develop the policies, structures, and interventions that ensure that all students can succeed regardless of their circumstances. For college and university administrators, the failure of their campuses to do so raises serious questions about whether they can fulfill their promise to provide access and opportunity.

TABLE 4.4. *Select analyses from* Learning from High-Performing and Fast-Gaining Institutions

Campus	Analysis	Impact
Florida State University	Year-to-year retention rates	Contributed to increase in Pell graduation rates from 61 percent in 2005 to 72 percent in 2012
Georgia State University	Tracking the rate of second-year students who achieve sophomore standing	Increased the proportion of returning students who attained sophomore standing from 22 percent in 2000 to 67 percent in 2008
Virginia Commonwealth University	Impact of course withdrawals	Reduced time and excess credits to degree
University of Alabama	Rates of D, F, and W grades	Intentional redesign of the largest courses led to major improvements in student success rates in those courses
University of North Carolina at Greensboro	Data on success for students in different fields	Identification of 12 key factors affecting student retention, including not having declared a major by the end of the first year
University of Wisconsin-Eau Claire	Transcripts	Determination that half of students were off their academic paths

Source: Joseph Yeado, Kati Haycock, Rob Johnstone, and Priyadarshini Chaplot, *Learning from High-Performing and Fast-Gaining Institutions: Top 10 Analyses to Provoke Discussion and Action on College Completion* (Washington, DC: Education Trust, 2014), https://edtrust.org/wp-content/uploads/2013/10/PracticeGuide1.pdf.

One of the biggest changes that campuses must make is ensuring that data and analytics lead to actions that benefit students and promote equity. Of course, to be successful in this effort, institutions need to have the appropriate systems and institutional culture in place. Data need to be integrated and structured in ways that reveal patterns and trends related to the full cycle of student life and a campus culture of evidence based on people, processes, and technology must be constantly nurtured.

One increasingly popular way that colleges are using data to encourage student success is small communications nudges that prompt students to take actions that improve the likelihood of favorable academic outcomes.[26] Using leading student success indicators and measurement frameworks, institutions have begun to identify the individual and institutional barriers to students' academic progress. Today, enrollment managers, advisors, and faculty use integrated student data to take actions to persuade students to make choices that lead to success. Examples include using text messages, emails, and other prompts to remind them to visit the library or schedule an advising session. The College at Brockport (SUNY) has used nudges to reduce Satisfactory Academic Progress violations among minority students by 30% through targeted workshops, weekly emails, and text messages. Staying on track academically ensured that the students could continue to receive federal aid.[27] West Kentucky Community and Technical College sent emails to students that included peer testimonials that contributed to an increase in the likelihood that students would attend tutoring sessions by 34%.[28] Other examples include using nudges to increase financial aid applications, reduce student borrowing, improve time management, and reduce registration times.[29]

Proactive advising has also been enhanced by using data and analytics well. The University Innovation Alliance, a coalition of eleven campuses across the country, "brought to scale intensive, proactive coaching interventions that were shown to increase student retention by nine to fourteen percent."[30] This process included providing intensive advising and individualized degree maps for low-income and first-generation students, early and real-time alerts powered by data, and targeted advising interventions if a student veered off track. The program, Monitoring Advising Analytics to Promote Success (MAAPS), was designed to enhance and scale proactive coaching interventions, a practice that has been shown to increase student retention. At Georgia State University, the lead institution of the project, students who received proactive coaching interventions accumulated 1.20 more credits, a 3-percentage-point-higher credit success rate, and a 0.17-point-higher GPA in their first academic year.[31] In another example, twenty-six broad-access two- and four-year colleges across the country leveraged technology and data to redesign advising, resulting in personalized and just-in-time communication with students and new types of student supports.[32]

When such efforts all come together, the results can be staggering. As Timothy Renick notes, Georgia State University (GSU) successfully "developed and implemented predictive analytics and data-informed systems in advising, financial aid, and student support services" that increased the graduation rate of students seeking bachelor's degrees by 23%.[33] These efforts also reversed equity gaps. Today, Latinx and African American students graduate from GSU at higher rates than white students, and Pell-eligible students graduate at a higher rate than non-Pell students. These results occurred during a transition period for GSU that included a merger with Georgia Perimeter College (a community college), the loss of millions of dollars in state funding, the decision to broaden admissions criteria, and rapidly shifting demographics. Today, GSU uses 800 data-based risk factors that are tracked daily and have resulted in 300,000 student interventions.[34]

Looking Ahead: Student Affairs and Blended Learning

Until recently, the conversation about using data to improve student outcomes mostly focused on two key dimensions. One—grades and advising—is largely academic; the other—classroom and traditional course delivery models—is physical. These two lenses remain useful, but their utility has narrowed over time. As college leaders have begun to look ahead to anticipate how student needs will continue to evolve, two clear patterns have emerged: students want support services that promote their health and well-being and address basic needs (e.g., food, housing, financial insecurity), which are usually found in student affairs, and they want greater flexibility to access their education across various modalities. The successful college and university of the future will find ways to measure, assess, and adapt to student needs and expectations while remaining true to its mission and standards. To achieve this balance, leaders will need to engage their campuses in efforts to strengthen data capacity in these key areas.

Student Affairs

Increasingly, colleges and universities have become aware of the importance of the totality of the student experience, including experiences outside the classroom that can influence the likelihood of retention, persistence, and completion. For many years, users of these three traditional measures have focused on the stereotypical first-time, full-time student and have made assumptions about course preferences, which resources satisfy basic needs, and which services students want most.[35] Given the evolving composition of student bodies, however, these measures do not tell the full story. Colleges that focus only on retention, persistence, and completion are likely to be in the dark about why some students will succeed while others will not.[36] Table 4.5 provides modern measures of student needs that have not yet been globally adopted by colleges. Although the information on the table is not exhaustive, it provides a list of areas of measurement that can augment the traditional data lenses college leaders use to determine institutional effectiveness.

Evolving student needs and college-going behaviors will diminish the value of traditional measurement frameworks over time unless they are coupled with new quantitative and qualitative measures. These metrics can inform how college and uni-

TABLE 4.5. *Contemporary measures of student needs*

Topic	Description
Food security	In recent years, awareness of issues related to student food insecurity have widened due to efforts from the U.S. Department of Agriculture and the Hope Center, which releases its #RealCollege survey each year. In 2019, the survey found that 39% of respondents had been food insecure over the previous 30 days.[1]
Housing security and homelessness	The affordable housing crisis has become a national issue. According to Habitat for Humanity, "for households earning less than $30,000, 81% of renters and 64% of homeowners were cost burdened." These challenges play out disproportionately among communities of color. The Hope Center found that among college students, 46% of respondents had been housing insecure in the previous year and 17% of students were homeless during the time of the survey.[2]
Childcare and caregiving	The rate of parent learners continues to increase, as does the rate of multigenerational households. In 2021, 15% of community college students were single parents. This circumstance presents unique challenges to caregiving learners, who have numerous important life priorities to consider.[3]
Student mental health and well-being	The physical and mental health and well-being of students is an area of growing importance across higher education. More than 8 in 10 presidents indicated in a recent adult and continuing education survey that mental health and well-being has become a bigger priority in recent years, and 72% have reallocated resources to address it. Anxiety and depression are the most common issues they hear about, and they often rely on student affairs to ensure that students are being served.[4]
Engagement and satisfaction	Student engagement and satisfaction can make the difference between completing a degree or leaving college. In addition to the National Survey on Student Engagement, which includes dimensions such as participation in high-impact practices, advisement, and sense of belonging, many universities have begun fielding their own instruments to help understand the factors outside the classroom that contribute to student success.[5]

(continued)

TABLE 4.5. *(continued)*

Topic	Description
Transportation	Nicholas Hillman and Taylor Weichman noted the prevalence of education deserts in large swaths of the country that often lead students to rack up expensive transportation bills just to access an education. Strategies to help students mitigate these costs can make the difference between a student completing college and dropping out.[6]
Device and internet access	As colleges and universities make the strategic decision to offer programs and courses across diverse and blended modalities, many will encounter the digital divide, a major barrier to entry. Having a clear sense of whether students have appropriate devices and quality internet access can uncover hidden barriers to successfully taking courses and earning a degree.[7]

Source: Adapted from Melissa Blankstein and Christine Wolff-Eisenberg, *Measuring the Whole Student: Landscape Review of Traditional and Holistic Approaches to Community College Student Success* (New York: Ithaka S+R, 2020), https://doi.org/10.18665/sr.313888.

[1] Christine Baker-Smith, Vanessa Coca, Sara Goldrick-Rab, Elizabeth Looker, Brianna Richardson, and Tiffani Williams, *#RealCollege 2020: Five Years of Evidence on Campus Basic Needs Insecurity* (Philadelphia, PA: The Hope Center for College, Community, and Justice, last modified February 2020), https://hope4college.com/wp-content/uploads/2020/02/2019_RealCollege_Survey_Report.pdf.

[2] "2020 State of the Nation's Housing Report 4 Key Takeaways for 2021," Habitat for Humanity, n.d., https://www.habitat.org/costofhome/2020-state-nations-housing-report-lack-affordable-housing; Baker-Smith et al., *#RealCollege 2020*, 2.

[3] Louis Soares, Jonathan S. Gagliardi, and Christopher J. Nellum, *The Post-Traditional Learners Manifesto Revisited: Aligning Postsecondary Education with Real Life for Adult Student Success* (Washington, DC: American Council on Education, 2017), https://www.acenet.edu/Documents/The-Post-Traditional-Learners-Manifesto-Revisited.pdf; Aimee Picchi, "Modern Families: Multigenerational Households Are on the Rise, Thanks to Financial and Emotional Benefits," *USA Today*, July 16, 2020, https://www.usatoday.com/story/money/columnist/2020/07/16/multigenerational-households-rise-prepare-pros-and-cons/5447028002; "Fast Facts 2021," American Association of Community Colleges, n.d., https://www.aacc.nche.edu/research-trends/fast-facts.

[4] Hollie Chessman and Morgan Taylor, "College Student Mental Health and Well-Being: A Survey of Presidents," *Higher Education Today*, August 12, 2019, https://www.higheredtoday.org/2019/08/12/college-student-mental-health-well-survey-college-presidents.

[5] "What Does NSSE Do?" National Survey of Student Engagement, n.d., https://nsse.indiana.edu/nsse/about-nsse/index.html; "Student Experience Survey, Office of Institutional Research, City University of New York, n.d., https://www.cuny.edu/about/administration/offices/oira/institutional/surveys.

[6] Nicholas Hillman and Taylor Weichman, *Education Deserts: The Continued Significance of 'Place' in the Twenty-First Century* (Washington, DC: American Council on Education, 2016), https://www.acenet.edu/Documents/Education-Deserts-The-Continued-Significance-of-Place-in-the-Twenty-First-Century.pdf; Blankstein and Wolff-Eisenberg, *Measuring the Whole Student*.

[7] Blankstein and Wolff-Eisenberg, *Measuring the Whole Student*.

versity leaders can renew their institutions routinely and with intentionality.

Versatile Course Delivery

As more students juggle family responsibilities, work, finances, mental health and well-being, and access to the internet and reliable transportation, they will enroll in colleges that can meet their needs through realigned services. The growing preference of students for blended modalities that accommodate other life priorities has implications for how academic programs are offered.

The trend toward preference for more flexible learning environments had been progressing slowly over the last two decades, as students have sought versatile delivery models for attending college. During the pandemic, particularly in places with high population density, this trend accelerated as colleges converted entire academic portfolios from face-to-face to almost entirely online instruction, sometimes synchronously and other times asynchronously. This pattern is not going away.

Colleges and universities across the country worked hard to understand how the complete shift to remote learning during the COVID-19 pandemic would influence student preferences for learning moving forward. A recent national survey revealed that 46% of students wanted the choice to attend courses in person or online and 33% wanted access to online student support services.[37] These findings suggest that many students prefer the flexibility and convenience that hybrid courses and/or simultaneous delivery of multiple modalities for a single course (e.g., HyFlex) provide. Campuses should jump at the chance to offer blended academic programs and student supports because doing so will help institutions manage short-term risk; offer more customized experiences; and, if structured properly over the long term, set up the institution to offer the experience students have said they want. It will also help higher education institutions make ends meet during periods of state funding austerity. Over time, offering more hybrid and online programs will also help institutions transcend the limitations of their physical campuses and reach students across the nation and perhaps even internationally.

What also became clear during the pandemic was that the digital divide has persisted: some students' lack of access to laptops, tablets, and reliable wireless internet became glaringly apparent. Campuses must reckon with the convergence of inflexibility about course and program delivery and inequitable access to a high-quality experience. The reasons institutions must address these issues are manifold. First, students need different forms of reliable access to courses. Second, colleges are increasingly reliant on enrollment from populations that lack access to technology. Third, these concerns have implications for versatility in educational delivery. Together, these factors may privilege students of means and hurt the long-term ability of colleges to run balanced budgets. Colleges and universities are thus experiencing pressure to make courses and programs accessible using technology. As noted earlier in this chapter, measuring student access to technology and a reliable internet connection is very important.

Now is the time for colleges to develop the means to assess the disciplines and course types that are best suited for traditional and blended modalities. Colleges should assess the courses that lend themselves best to various instructional modes. Table 4.6 provides a sample of the course delivery matrix that institutions can create by engaging with their faculty, who know how ready specific course types are for diverse modalities.

However, simply building flexibility into courses and programs is insufficient. The quality of the educational experience needs to be equivalent across modalities. This underscores the importance of fostering enthusiasm about assessment of student learning outcomes. The combination of the development of new measurement frameworks that focus on student needs and the demand for more flexible course offerings can yield new forms of data that create a more accurate picture of the factors that influence student success. Senior campus leaders must emphasize the

TABLE 4.6. *Degree to which specific course types lend themselves to various modalities*

Course type	Fully online	Hybrid	Fully face to face
Lecture	H	H	L
Seminar	M	M	M
Recitation	L	L	H
Lab	L	L	H
Clinical or practicum	L	M	H
Field study	L	M	H
Internship	L	H	H
Independent study	H	H	L
Supplemental instruction or tutorial	H	H	H

Note: L = low, M = medium, H = high.

importance of these issues and invest resources in collecting quality and consistent data over time. In the future, more data and better technology will likely result in more personalized prescriptions that target specific students' individual needs.

Conclusion

By clearly defining an aspiration that prioritizes student success and equity, senior campus leaders can convince a campus to elevate the institution to new heights by serving students as they pursue their dreams. Data and analytics can help make an aspiration real for faculty and staff, the people who can turn an aspiration into a reality. When data is integrated across multiple dimensions, campus stakeholders can begin to translate big goals into specific steps. Disaggregating and analyzing integrated data by student characteristics can help faculty and staff see how they can effect transformational change that results in equitable access and equitable outcomes.

The patterns and trends that surface when integrated data is disaggregated and analyzed are the foundation for efforts to create or renew institutional practices and policies in ways that encourage and support students as they navigate increasingly complex pathways to a degree. This shift is an important milestone on the analytics journey of a college or university. When presidents and senior campus leaders convince data users across the institution to use the spectrum of descriptive and predictive analyses in ways that promote action, they position the campus to meet the needs of an ever more diverse student population. They also position their institutions to continually maintain and renew their vitality, something that is increasingly difficult given the myriad pressures the higher education sector is facing. The reality is that colleges and universities can increase their financial sustainability by effectively serving historically underserved students New forms of data in key areas can help put colleges at a competitive advantage while serving students better—a win-win for presidents and provosts. However, finding the resources to appropriately fund these efforts requires a focus on strategic finance.

Chapter 5

Strategic Finance and Resource Optimization

The success of a modern institution depends on its ability to effectively generate, invest, and manage resources in ways that promote equitable access and outcomes and position a college or university for a sustainable future by investing in what matters most to the institution. This undertaking is complex because external factors have generated new and more intense pressures that interact with colleges and universities in potentially disruptive ways. The interaction of external pressures with internal structures has put the higher education financial model in a state of flux. The increasing unreliability of traditional revenue sources, including state funding, and an ongoing affordability crisis have introduced new levels of uncertainty, prompting college presidents and senior campus leaders to reconsider how their campus approaches strategic finance.

Faculty and staff need to use financial data in tandem with performance data to understand cost and performance in relation to the institution's strategic direction and identity. Class size and fill rates, the distribution and opportunity cost of release time, program margins, activity-based costing, energy savings, and the success rates of grantmaking activity are just some of the critical areas that drive the bottom line. In order for leaders to fully understand financial costs and benefits, users across campus need to integrate financial data into the infrastructure. Few institutions have fully achieved this arrangement. This chapter outlines key strategies for developing and using integrated financial data.

The Impact of Economic Volatility on Postsecondary Institutions

In an era of financial uncertainty, demographic shifts, challenges related to college affordability, and changing priorities of state legislatures, colleges and universities across the country are rethinking their approach to strategic finance. Now more than ever, institutions must generate, effectively allocate, and manage resources in support of the students they serve without the expectation of reliable external funding. All too often, these circumstances mean doing more with less and working on razor-thin margins that put a typical institution in a state of financial vulnerability. This has been an issue for some time, as evidenced by an increase in campus closures and mergers, and it will become more prominent in the aftermath of the COVID-19 pandemic.

Drivers of Volatility

More than a decade since the onset of the Great Recession of 2008–2009, institutions are still adjusting to greater financial volatility. In 2019, the University of Alaska narrowly avoided a 41% cut in state appropriations of $136 million, although it could not stave off $70 million in line-item spending cuts spread out over multiple fiscal years.[1] In 2016 and 2017, higher education in Illinois suffered substantial declines in higher education funding because of a prolonged budget standoff between the state legislature and the governor.[2] Louisiana and Wisconsin have also experienced decreases in education appropriations because funding has not changed in response to increased enrollment.[3] The end result is "significantly diminished per-student funding for higher education."[4] In fact, according to the State Higher Education Executive Officers, students now fund more than half of their higher education.[5]

The Consequences of Volatility

According to William Doyle, Amberly Dziesinski, and Jennifer Delaney, institutions experiencing financial volatility face difficult challenges. They can raise tuition, but that might hurt overall enrollment. They may also find it difficult to hire and retain faculty. As Doyle, Dziesinski, and Delaney point out, "lack of knowledge about future levels of funding makes planning for staffing levels difficult, if not impossible."[6]

Other studies have noted the shift in public higher education from a reliance on state appropriations to other and more diversified revenue streams.[7] Decreases in state appropriations limit the ability of institutions to diversify their revenue streams beyond tuition and fees. One study explains why: "In many cases, endowment spending rules and hesitancy on the part of administrators to spend down endowment principal meant that these funds were largely ineffective in balancing unanticipated shortfalls, especially given that endowment earnings were negatively influenced by the same changes in economic conditions driving state budgetary shortfalls."[8] Financially constrained institutions can also reduce investment and hiring, but both of these measures can negatively impact student outcomes and decrease the quality of academic programs and student support services.[9] Fiscal uncertainty can also reduce the likelihood that risk-averse private funders will be willing to cover part of an institution's structural fiscal gap. Identifying volatility drivers is one of the first things senior campus leaders can do to position themselves to refresh their approach to strategic finance. These influences will vary to a certain degree based on location, campus traits, student body composition, and other factors.

Case Study: Drivers of Volatility in New York State

According to the New York State Education Department's Office of Higher Education directory, New York, the fourth most populous state in the country, has 350 postsecondary campuses. New York State has ten distinct regions, ranging from New York City, the largest city in the country, to small cities in the southern tier of the state to rural communities in the North Country to the Capital Region, which includes the cities of Albany, Schenectady, Troy, and Saratoga. While postsecondary institutions in these regions each face local challenges, they also share many difficulties.

Population Loss

From 2010 to 2020, New York State's population grew 0.43% per year, below the average median year-over-year growth rate of 0.47% for 2011–2020.[10] Census Bureau estimates indicate that New York was one of only nine states to experience a population decline from July 1, 2017 to July 1, 2018.[11] Even New York City's population declined 0.50% from 2016 to 2018, when the number of people who left the city surpassed the combined number of births and international immigrants.[12]

Similar trends have been observed in other states in the Northeast and Midwest in both urban and rural areas. These patterns shape how colleges and universities approach strategic finance because people are leaving these states for a number of reasons, including the climate and an overall tax burden of 13.04%, which is highest in the nation.[13] This exodus is detrimental to state tax revenues and opportunities for employment, and it has a corrosive effect on the ability of a state to remain financially sustainable.

A Graying Population and the Medicaid Pinch

As the population continues to age and decrease, the expansion of programs such as Medicaid, the third largest mandatory program in the federal budget, puts increasing pressure on states.[14] States like New York, which receives the lowest federal matching rate of 50%, will experience greater pressures due to shifting demographics.[15] From 2007 to 2017, the number of New Yorkers aged 65 and older increased by 26%; this age group now accounts for 19% of the state's population.[16] Moreover, the number of New Yorkers aged 85 and older increased 26% during the same time frame.[17] The aging population of the state will lead to an increase in Medicaid obligations and in all likelihood a decrease in higher education funding.

Closing Doors

A combination of policy changes and cultural and political hostility has had negative effects on immigration. New administrative hurdles for international students, including an increase in student application fees, greater enforcement of visa conditions, and scrutiny over permit programs, are creating a chilling effect on study in the United States, especially in states such as New York that rely heavily on immigration to maintain stable populations.[18] From 2016-17 to 2020-21, the number of new international enrollments at US colleges and universities decreased by 45.6%.[19]

If these trends continue, competition for international students could intensify. Institutions could also experience loss of tuition revenue because international students typically pay more than domestic and in-state students. At institutions such as Wright State University in Dayton, Ohio; the University of Central Missouri; and Kansas State University, Trump administration policies implemented in 2020 required international students to take on-campus courses in order to remain in the country. While the Biden administration has since begun addressing issues related to international student visas, the impact of earlier policies will have negative residual effects on college budgets for many years.

Many institutions across the country have experienced volatility drivers similar to those in New York state. Many of these external pressures have worsened significantly because of the COVID-19 pandemic and are likely to persist for several years at least. Colleges and universities throughout the United States will not be able to rely on old rules of thumb, such as countercyclical enrollment growth in response to an economic recession, unless they pivot quickly to offer quality academic and student support experiences in fully online or hybrid forms in order to attract and retain more students. Data can provide the foundation for an agile framework as institutions respond to rapid and unprecedented change.

Strategic Finance

Strategic finance refers to an intentional effort by a college or university to generate and distribute resources in ways that support aspirations focused on student success, equity, and institutional sustainability. The thoughtful creation and allocation of resources works best when senior campus leaders take a data-informed approach. However, a number of institutional barriers may stand in the way.

Like other efforts, a data-informed approach to strategic finance suffers from a lack of integration in terms of both organizational divisions and data infrastructure. In fact, the latter is reflective of the former—many problems with imperfect or incomplete data stem from an inadequate organizational structure and/or culture. For example, business officers often operate in their own bubble and are often left out of discussions and decisions related to academic affairs and student success. This disconnect has caused academic affairs and student success divisions to be less informed about the costs associated with delivering programs and services and the revenues associated with increased student success. Since large portions of institutional budgets are tied up in academic affairs and student success efforts, this lack of understanding slows efforts to use resources in an optimal way.

The combination of a lack of integrated leadership and organizational and cultural divides separate integrated data from the people who can use it to its greatest effect. The result is that colleges and universities are ill equipped to make sense of financial data and the very systems and people who can generate insights from it have little knowledge of or training about how best to do so. If colleges and universities are to overcome the many and complex financial challenges they now face, they must build bridges between the academic and financial sides of the institution. Very few campuses can afford to continue in such a disintegrated way.

Recognizing the need to break down institutional silos in order to create an integrated approach to data analytics, the National Association of College and University Business Officers (NACUBO) has prioritized encouraging higher education institutions to integrate data and analytics in order to achieve strategic goals.[20] In 2019, chief business officers cited strategic thinking and decision-making as one of the most critical aspects of their jobs, which means that they can no longer operate in a bubble.[21] That year, NACUBO's Analytics Advisory Group, which consists of business officers and other higher education leaders, began supporting advancing data-informed decision-making.[22] In addition to sharing research and case studies to highlight best practices, the group provides resources that offer guidance about how to collaborate with the other side of the institution.[23]

Understanding the Business Model

In order to take an integrated approach to strategic finance, institutions need to thoroughly analyze their business models. In many sectors, a business model describes how a person or a company plans to make money.[24] That definition cannot apply to a college or university because at its core, a higher education institution is a public good with massive tangible and intangible benefits.[25] Within the context of higher education, a business model focuses on elements such as value propositions, resources, processes, and revenue formulas.[26] These elements are interdependent, and if they are properly designed, they work together to enable an institution to operate in keeping with its unique identity in a financially responsible way.

Perhaps the most distinguishing trait of a higher education business model that it is driven by balance and sustainability, not profits. An institution that focused on profits above all else would be anathema in the context of the culture of American higher education (although there are some glaring exceptions in the for-profit sector). Making profits the bottom line would result in a slash-and-burn exercise that would include academic disciplines and programs. That outcome would be a tragedy. Programs such as history, philosophy, and sociology offer the same value as engineering, biomedicine, and data science, especially if you look carefully at the skills and competencies that each teaches and the long-term outcomes for the workforce. Programs in the social sciences also cost less and often cross-subsidize more expensive majors. That is, after all, the point of the higher education business model: a balanced approach to sustaining a rich arrangement of programs and services that is greater than the sum of its parts.

A Measurement Framework for Strategic Finance

Given the mounting financial volatility higher education is experiencing, institutions are looking for ways to squeeze the most from scarce resources without sacrificing academic quality or cutting student support services or mission-critical programs. Better and more integrated data that span academic and administrative functions in ways that connect programs, performance, cost, and revenues are key to catalyzing strategic finance at any given campus. Recently, rpk GROUP, a consulting and advisory firm in higher education, developed a measurement framework to help colleges and universities catalyze strategic finance across multiple dimensions, including affordability, revenue and spending, efficiency, and outcomes.[27]

Affordability

Try as they might, many institutions have reached a point where they can no longer absorb the full brunt of decreased state funding. The result has been a steep increase in the sticker price of college. According to *Trends in College Pricing*, from 1989-90 to 2019-20, tuition and fees tripled at public four-year institutions and more than doubled at public two-year and private not-for-profit four-year institutions, after adjusting for inflation (table 5.1).[28]

This significant change highlights affordability as a critical component of the sustainability of campuses. If students cannot afford to come, it matters very little whether the education is

TABLE 5.1. *Average tuition and fees and room and board (enrollment-weighted) 1989-90 to 2019-20, selected years (in 2019 dollars)*

| Academic year | Tuition and fees only | | | Tuition and fees plus room and board | |
	Private not-for-profit four-year	Public four-year	Public two-year	Private not-for-profit four-year	Public four-year
1989-90	$17,860	$3,510	$1,730	$25,900	$9,730
1999-00	$23,890	$5,170	$2,540	$33,060	$12,440
2009-10	$30,670	$8,420	$3,060	$41,780	$18,160
2019-20	$36,880	$10,440	$3,730	$49,870	$21,950
Percent change	206	297	216	193	226

Source: Jennifer Ma, Sandy Baum, Matea Pender, and CJ Libassi, *Trends in College Pricing: 2019* (New York, NY: College Board), 12, figure 3, https://research.collegeboard.org/pdf/trends-college-pricing-2019-full-report.pdf.

impactful and high quality. Measures of affordability should focus on the factors that promote or hinder students' access to college and student success. Table 5.2 describes various ways to measure this crucial component of higher education strategic finance.

Measures of affordability can help colleges and universities ensure that students are not priced out of attending without lowering price to a point that puts the institution in the red. They can also be used to inform students and help them feel more financially secure and confident about continuing to pursue a quality college credential. This mindset is obviously beneficial to both the student and the campus. Looking at affordability is just one dimension of institutional sustainability, however. Colleges and universities must also use data to track revenues and spending and to identify inefficiencies that, if eliminated, could free up resources that could be reinvested.

Revenues, Spending, and Efficiency

The sustainability of any college's financial model often relies on a balanced portfolio of academic programs and support service. It is also true that, given the fact that the bulk of college budgets are tied up in personnel costs that are often fixed and difficult to pivot, institutions need to be mindful about how they maintain a positive balance sheet. For most campuses, this boils down to two dimensions: the total revenues and expenses per student and staffing, which typically accounts for 75% to 95% of a college's budget. Some important measures are noted in table 5.3.

Especially after the COVID-19 pandemic, institutions are preparing for sharp declines in state support and enrollment, which means that even more creative approaches to optimizing resources and diversifying funding streams will be needed. One strategy is to ensure that faculty are teaching courses near full capacity, which helps institutions get the most out of their current teaching capacity and potentially accrue resources that can be reinvested into academic excellence and student success.

TABLE 5.2. *Affordability measures*

Metrics	Definitions
Tuition and fees (in-district)	Annual tuition and required fees for full-time students. At public institutions this reflects the in-state or in-district charges.
Net price: total	Average annual price for full-time, first-time degree/ certificate undergraduate students who were awarded grant or scholarship aid: total cost of attendance minus federal, state, local, or institutional grant aid. Cost of attendance = published tuition and required fees, room and board, books and supplies, and other expenses.
Net price: low-income students ($0-$30k)	Average annual price for full-time, first-time degree/certificate undergraduate students with family incomes of $30,000 or less who were awarded grant or scholarship aid: total cost of attendance minus federal, state, local, or institutional grant aid. Cost of attendance = published tuition and required fees, room and board, books and supplies, and other expenses.
Percent students with Pell grants	Number of full-time, first-time degree-seeking undergraduate students awarded Pell grants divided by total number of full-time, first-time degree-seeking undergraduate students.
Percent students with federal loans	Number of full-time, first-time degree-seeking undergraduate students awarded federal loans divided by total number of full-time, first-time degree-seeking undergraduate students.
Percent students with institutional grant aid	Number of full-time, first-time degree-seeking undergraduate students awarded institutional grant aid divided by total number of full-time, first-time degree-seeking undergraduate students.
Average institutional grant	Total institutional grant aid (scholarships/fellowships) awarded to full-time, first-time degree-seeking undergraduate students divided by total number of students receiving institutional grants.
Institutional grant aid per FTE[a] student	Total institutional grant aid (scholarships/fellowships) awarded by the institution divided by number of FTE students.
Tuition discount rate	Total institutional grant aid divided by the sum of net tuition and fee revenue plus total institutional grant aid.

Source: rpk GROUP, "Model—Strategic Finance Dashboard," Adopting a Strategic Finance Lens, 2020, accessed October 5, 2020, http://rpkgroup.com/adopting-a-strategic-finance-lens.
[a] Full-time equivalent.

TABLE 5.3. *Revenue and spending measures*

Metrics	Definitions
Total revenue (net) per FTE student	Sum of total revenue (net tuition revenue; federal, state, and local appropriations, grants, and contracts; private and affiliated gifts, grants, contracts), including auxiliaries, hospitals, and other independent operations divided by number of FTE students. (Investment returns are excluded because they include unrealized gains and reflect volatility in the financial markets.)
Total spending per FTE student	Sum of education and general spending (instruction, student services, research, academic support, institutional support, operations and maintenance, and grants) and spending of auxiliaries, hospitals, and independent operations divided by number of FTE students.
Education-related spending per FTE student	E&R[a] expenses: instruction, student services, and a pro-rata share of overhead, which includes academic and institutional support and operations and maintenance (for institutions without research or public service expenditures, then all the overhead costs are captured in E&R) divided by number of FTE students.
Tuition-financed share of student spending (student share of spending)	Net tuition and fees revenue divided by total E&R spending.
Compensation spending per FTE employee	Total compensation outlay (salaries and benefits) for all employees divided by number of FTE employees.

Source: rpk GROUP, "Strategic Finance Dashboard," Adopting a Strategic Finance Lens, 2020, accessed October 5, 2020, http://rpkgroup.com/adopting-a-strategic-finance-lens.
[a] Education and related.

A word of caution: these measures can create a threat narrative and evoke fear among campus constituents, so they need to be used with care, and their intended use needs to be positively framed and effectively communicated. If not, people who run small programs or services that serve a limited number of students or clients may feel that their roles are under the micro-

TABLE 5.4. *Efficiency measures*

Metrics	Definitions
Faculty throughput	Total undergraduate and graduate credit hours (including contact hours converted to credit hours) divided by number of full-time equivalent faculty
Student-to-faculty ratio	Number of full-time equivalent students divided by number of full-time equivalent faculty

Source: rpk GROUP, "Strategic Finance Dashboard," Adopting a Strategic Finance Lens, 2020, accessed October 5, 2020, http://rpkgroup.com/adopting-a-strategic-finance-lens.

scope, as they often serve a small number of students at a high cost. The steps presidents and campus leaders take to maximize revenues, reduce expenses, and optimize resources need to be done wisely and delicately. Measures of revenues, expenses, and efficiency should not be used to eliminate programs unless circumstances are exceptionally dire. Instead, these activities should be used to determine whether opportunities exist for scalable programs that generate positive outcomes in cost-effective ways.

Outcomes

People outside an institution will judge it according to how effectively it helps students earn a high-quality degree or credential. Those inside the institution know that this goal must be achieved within the constraints of a finite pool of resources. Basic measures that tell senior campus leaders whether spending and credits per completion are trending upward or downward are very useful and easy to communicate.

Measures related to outcomes help create a deeper understanding of the costs of doing business, particularly when they are disaggregated by program or unit and when they are coupled with measures of equity. When costs per degree in one program are higher than in another program, it leads campus leaders to ask why. If credits per degree are misaligned with the stated

TABLE 5.5. *Outcomes*

Metrics	Definitions
Spending per completion (degree/certificate)	Total spending (E&R[a]) divided by total number of completions (degrees, certificates, and other awards)
Spending per credit hour	Total spending (E&R) divided by total number of undergraduate and graduate credit hours (including any contact hours converted to credit hours)
Completions per $100,000 of total spending	Total completions (degrees, certificates, and other awards) divided by total spending (E&R) multiplied by 100,000
Completions per 100 FTE[b] students	Total completions (degrees, certificates, and other awards) divided by number of full-time equivalent students multiplied by 100
Student credit hours per completion	Undergraduate student credit hours divided by total number of undergraduate completions (degrees and other awards)

Source: rpk GROUP, "Strategic Finance Dashboard," Adopting a Strategic Finance Lens, 2020, accessed October 5, 2020, http://rpkgroup.com/adopting-a-strategic-finance-lens.
[a] Education and related.
[b] Full-time equivalent.

credit requirement for a degree, then opportunities exist to examine the nature of excess credit accumulation to determine if there are inefficiencies that can simultaneously free up resources and create a smoother path to a degree for students.

Approaches to Integration

Taking a strategic approach to finance, including the integration and widespread use of financial data, student data, and program and unit data, helps colleges and universities deepen their understanding of the relationship between where and how resources are allocated and institutional effectiveness. A framework based on affordability, revenues and expenses, efficiency, and outcomes should be applied clearly and consistently to the broader institution and to individual academic, student support, and administrative programs. It should be done in an empowering way. It should also be developed with a broad cross-section of campus constituencies and through consensus, which can create a compelling case for transformational change. In recent years, institutions such as the University of California, Riverside, and California State University, Fullerton, have adopted activities-based costing and smart budgeting with great success. These multi-staged cost allocation methodologies measure the costs associated with academic and administrative programs. A key piece of their success is that they set aside some of the savings for reinvestment in the programs that generated them. These kinds of incentives are vital to creating an appetite for change and for a data-informed approach to managing and improving the efficiency and effectiveness of programs.[29]

Even if a measurement framework or particular program offers promise, senior campus leaders need to take action to turn value propositions into reality. Integrated data are needed that help illustrate the relationship between productivity and cost if programs and services are to have maximum impact. Deans, department chairs, and advisors could all benefit from data and analytics.

Conclusion

External pressures, such as growing inequality, changing priorities of state legislatures, demographic shifts, and calls for greater efficiency and accountability have introduced financial uncertainty for colleges and universities nationwide. Understanding these external pressures and their impact on the higher education business model is a vital component of a modern approach to strategic finance.

Achieving the balance between growth and fiscal responsibility is a difficult task that requires campus leaders to understand the factors that impact financial situation of their institution. Through open dialogue, senior campus leaders can make the strategic finance process clearer to their campus constituencies. They should welcome questions and constructive dialogue and recognize support and participation from campus constituents. Campus stakeholders can work together to innovate and collaborate and, in doing so, develop creative solutions that ensure quality, promote investment, enhance the classroom experience, and make it possible for their institutions to continue to function as cohesive and sustainable communities that drive progress and success for students and the public they serve.

Chapter 6

Academic Quality and Renewal

A community of teachers and scholars and an innovative, robust, and contemporary curriculum are crucial components of a healthy college. The richness and relevance of academic programs and scholarship weigh heavily on the minds of many prospective students and their families, employers, and legislatures when making decisions about whether to attend, partner with, or support an institution. Some students are preoccupied with obtaining a credential that will help them meet minimum requirements for a job. The ability of an academic program to help students in whatever their pursuits may be is often a good indicator of the health of an institution. Today, a heightened emphasis on postgraduate outcomes, assessment and continuous improvement, and fluid transfer and a growing reliance on contingent faculty have raised concerns that the academic core of a campus is changing in fundamental and perhaps detrimental ways. Campuses can use data and analytics in support of maintaining academic programs, understanding the expectations of students, and addressing the needs of employers and lawmakers.

Leaders who can facilitate the adoption of a comprehensive and flexible approach to using evidence within academic programs can promote the academic health of an institution because such an approach will help departments and programs reach their full potential. More and more, colleges that use data to renew and align academic programs can avoid the difficult and expensive process of creating new programs from scratch or disbanding others completely. This chapter outlines how campus leaders can engage their departments in the use of analytics as a tool to enhance and preserve their institution's academic identity.

Pockets of Excellence and Uneven Spaces in Data Use

Colleges and universities have always had pockets of excellence regarding the use of data and a culture of evidence. Offices of institutional research, institutional effectiveness, and assessment have led the way in collaboration with faculty. These stakeholders have kept institutions squarely focused on answering the question, Are our students learning? Whether institutions want to make sure they satisfy the requirements for accreditation, provide quality academic programs and student services, or promote equity, they would be remiss if they ignored the growing importance of creative and innovative approaches to continuous improvement.

Efforts of campuses to become better and more accountable require approaches that offer equal breadth and depth. Analyses like those highlighted in chapter 4 offer solid breadth. Reviewing grade patterns in course sections are incredibly useful, but they represent only a composite of student outcomes.[1] Using analyses like those noted in table 4.3 optimally requires a close look at the data to see where students are experiencing difficulty learning. This is where assessment comes in. Yet although conversations surrounding how to best use big data and analytics to promote evidence-based, equity-driven transformations have gained momentum, similar discussions about the evolving nature of assessment have lagged.[2] Luckily, the National Institute for Learning Outcomes Assessment and other key stakeholders have noticed the lack of attention to assessments.

This recognition has led to a sharper focus on equitable assessments, which focuses on opportunities for improving teaching practices instead of on identifying the perceived deficits of students. Some notable examples of equitable assessment efforts are included in table 6.1.

Equitable assessment focuses on understanding assessment practices and methods through the eyes of students. This helps eliminate unintended biases that assessment leads may introduce. This type of assessment is accomplished by gathering diverse perspectives—both from different teams and administrative units and from members of the college community who are racially and ethnically diverse—throughout all stages of the process, a practice that promotes inclusion and a sense of belonging. Data are collected in a manner that can be disaggregated by important student traits. Where gaps exist, diverse teams analyze the findings with a focus on identifying structural and pedagogical deficits instead of focusing on the limitations of students. In many ways, these key themes mirror broader approaches to the use of big data and analytics and represent promising developments in using assessment to promote equitable outcomes while ensuring academic quality.

Across the country and even within individual campuses, there are pockets of excellence in which faculty and staff use data effectively to strengthen teaching, learning, and support; promote excellence in research, scholarship, and creative works; and maintain a diverse and relevant curriculum. Within these same campuses a great deal of unevenness also exists. It is fairly common for a faculty to include both standout professors who

TABLE 6.1. *Modern approaches to equitable assessment*

Institution	Rubric	Key components
Wake Forest University	Campus life	Campus life includes participant feedback throughout the assessment process, including measures and analysis. Diverse and multidisciplinary assessment teams carefully choose and/or create conceptual models. Assessment items that are applicable across groups are used, and diverse student perspectives are included through inclusive recruitment and sampling. Awareness and consideration of potential barriers to access and completion of assessments are considered, and strong protocols ensure privacy and security of data. There is a commitment to fairness in interpretation and analysis and fair resource allocation based on evidence. The relevance of assessment feedback to participants is also considered.[1]
San Diego State University	Commuter student support	The entire institution is committed to organizational decision-making based on helping students achieve their full potential regardless of their background. Outcomes-based assessments are aligned with equity performance indicators (learning outcomes rooted in students' personal, social, cognitive, and behavioral skills). Students' lived experiences are integrated in all assessment methods, and assessment data are interrogated for differentiated opportunities to repair inequities and promote more equitable outcomes. Data and findings are contextualized by including and listening to diverse student perspectives and feedback.[2]
Cornell University	Ripple Effect Mapping	Ripple Effect Mapping is a group evaluation method that engages program and community stakeholders retrospectively and visually maps chains of effects. It is iterative and inclusive and involves appreciative inquiry, a participatory approach, interactive group interviewing and reflection, and mind mapping in an effort to identify material outcomes. The stories and voices of diverse stakeholders are integrated into the process and are given equal validity. Data are disaggregated in order to understand the experiences of marginalized or minoritized students. Emphasis is placed on understanding outcomes as defined by those served, in contrast to traditional methods that are biased by the perspectives of project leads.[3]

Portland State University	General education	Students are invited to demonstrate their learning in activities beyond the classroom and community-based learning is embedded in all general education courses. All students in first-year and sophomore general education courses are supported by a peer mentor. At the end of the year, first-year students create electronic portfolios that include a reflection and assignments related to learning goals. Students choose the evidence and results are disaggregated by student subgroups. Together, student choice and disaggregation support equitable assessment. Faculty are engaged in a collegial process of discussion and review regardless of rank. They are invited, not mandated, to participate. Steps are taken to ensure adjunct involvement, including compensation for participation in review and assessment.[4]

---

[1] Nicole Brocato, Matthew Clifford, Nelson Brunsting, and José Villalba, *Wake Forest University: Campus Life and Equitable Assessment*, Equity Case Study (Urbana, IL: National Institute for Learning Outcomes Assessment, 2021), https://www.learningoutcomesassessment.org/wp-content/uploads/2021/02/EquityCase-WFU-2.pdf.

[2] Erick Montenegro, *San Diego State University: Supporting Commuter Students through Equity-Driven and Student-Focused Assessment*, Equity Case Study (Urbana, IL: National Institute for Learning Outcomes Assessment, 2020), https://www.learningoutcomesassessment.org/wp-content/uploads/2020/10/EquityCase-SDSU.pdf.

[3] Leslie Meyerhoff, *Cornell University: Ripple Effect Mapping*, Equity Case Study (Urbana, IL: National Institute for Learning Outcomes Assessment, 2020), https://www.learningoutcomesassessment.org/wp-content/uploads/2020/06/Cornell-Equity-Case.pdf.

[4] Rowanna Carpenter, Vicki Reitenauer, and Aimee Shattuck, "Portland State University: General Education and Equitable Assessment," *Equity Case Study* (June 2020), https://www.learningoutcomesassessment.org/wp-content/uploads/2020/06/Portland-Equity-Case.pdf.

are expert teachers and productive scholars and those who are behind the curve in one or both areas. Often, one variable that separates the good from the bad is a commitment to using data and analytics.

Certain academic majors or departments seem to be leaders in using data to revisit and refresh their curriculum in ways that appeal to both students and employers. These exemplars often share a few distinguishing characteristics. They are aware of available data and continue to learn about relevant methodologies as they develop. They use a measurement framework that includes a process for setting targets that feeds into the institution's aspirational and strategic goals, learning outcomes, and student learning objectives. Such frameworks are often implicit in an institution's culture of evidence and are often made more apparent through accreditation self-studies or external reviews. A comprehensive assessment framework should be well established and routinely monitored with an eye on the trend line. These goals, outcomes, and objectives should be strategic, measurable, actionable, achievable, and time bound and they should be difficult to rig. While this framework may seem like common sense, the truth is that concepts rarely get implemented successfully in a college without substantial revision from the stakeholders who are being asked to adopt them, given their unique knowledge of the realities faculty, students, and staff face on the ground. Gathering input into how things are measured and analyzed from data users across campus helps ensure that the implementation and adoption of analytics will succeed and nurtures a culture of evidence.

Too often, the use of data and analytics in pursuit of a unified vision for success breaks down between college constituents across various programs, divisions, and departments, despite good intentions. The reasons can include differences in priorities and incentives among leaders at different levels of the institution; a lack of capable leadership in individual schools and departments; and narrow definitions of success that are siloed, disorganized, and infrequently measured.

Differences in Stakeholder Priorities Influence
How Data Are Used

A culture of evidence needs to reach deep into the organization if colleges and universities are to serve students well and remain sustainable during periods of disruption. Alignment and consistency between senior campus leaders is a requirement, but they are insufficient by themselves. Achieving and maintaining alignment and consistency become harder the deeper one travels down an organizational chart because all organizations have natural points where they diffuse. This phenomenon is especially true of academe. The pursuit of organizational alignment and consistency is most vulnerable in areas where institutions go from a handful of divisions and schools to dozens of administrative units and academic departments. It is at this point where the differences between campus leaders regarding using data become visible. Efforts to scale out data analytics often wither when data focus on the aggregate. That level of information is helpful to the highest levels of college and university leadership, but it lacks sufficient granularity to offer value to department chairs and program directors.

Presidents, provosts, and deans are nomadic creatures who follow a mission from place to place as they climb the leadership ranks. This journey exposes them to different ways of doing things, and along the way they often become change agents who have become loyal to their field instead of to a singular campus, school, or department. They are administrators, not faculty, and they are rightfully unapologetic about their desire facilitate improvement. Data are a means to that end.

In contrast, department chairs have an entirely different orientation. First and foremost, they are faculty. Most plan to spend the rest of their careers in the department they currently lead. They are union members if one exists at their college, and they know to toe the line. Typically elected by peers with whom they share deeply personal bonds, chairs see their department as a family tree, not an organizational chart. If circumstances change drastically under their watch, conditions can get uncomfortable when they return to their faculty role. So department chairs are often on the front line of trying to sustain the status quo at a college. They are more likely to tinker at the edges than to pursue transformational change. When their provost or a dean talks to them about using data for the greater good, they usually want to know what is in it for their department. After all, if they are asked to use data today, what will come next? An accountability framework? Activities-based costing? Zero-sum budgeting? These ideas do benefit the overall health of a campus and are all worthy of consideration, but they are also tough sells. When a department chair or program director buys in to data analytics, it is incumbent upon senior leadership to provide tools and training to help them do so successfully.

Tough Transitions and Uneven Institutional Investment

Department chairs are uniquely positioned to help an institution improve, but campus leaders need to support them so they have the resources to fill that role. They are very capable of doing their job well, but they face unique challenges, particularly during the transition from faculty member to chair. The jump from being an academic focused on their own teaching, research, and scholarship to managing an entire department is rough. Department chairs focus on representing their department to the administration; maintaining a conducive work climate; developing long-range goals; recruiting and retaining faculty; enhancing teaching quality; managing department resources; overseeing tenure, promotion, and review; and teaching and advising students—all while trying to maintain scholarship and work-life balance and dealing with an endless backlog of work.[3]

Department chairs typically do not receive formal training for what is often their first leadership role on campus. According to Walter Gmelch and colleagues, 67% of chairs receive no formal training from their institutions, and those who do get ten hours or fewer. Most department chairs feel that the training they receive is inadequate.[4] It takes time for chairs to acquire the hard and soft skills they need to succeed. However, nine-month faculty contracts and an average term of four years in the role mean that by the time chairs are seasoned veterans, their tenure is ending. These challenges are further amplified by the reality that the process of becoming a chair is political, not competitive: becoming a chair is more of a popularity contest than a decision based on who is best prepared to do the job. This tendency makes formal training for department chairs incredibly important. Whether that training is focused on budgets, performance versus institutional goals, or research, the one common theme is that chairs need to be familiar with and comfortable using campus data.

Helping Chairs Facilitate Successful Departments

Well-equipped department chairs can make or break an institution because of their collective strategic and financial weight. Given the high stakes of operating a college, deans and provosts are acutely interested in making sure that the choices chairs make are based on evidence. The high-level measurement frameworks campus executives use are not as useful for chairs, however. As they work to create a standardized approach among departments, provosts and deans often introduce measurement frameworks they have learned about from their experiences (often at other campuses) or through professional networks. This process usually does not go well, in part because if it came from elsewhere, there is no way it could ever fully capture the distinctiveness of the institution, let alone individual departments. Although *something* beneficial can be gleaned from how other colleges use data, the tools provosts and deans use are probably too macro to offer any tangible benefit to department chairs.

The solution is to find more granular metrics that advance the goals of schools within universities or colleges and departments within those schools. As with most initiatives at an institution, this effort requires collaboration and compromise. If discussion and analysis yields a set of goals that are clearly defined and are based on sources that all stakeholders can see and if stakeholders agree that achieving those goals will move the needle for the institution, then the effort is off to a positive start. Trust is established when promised incentives are delivered that are based on positive trends that are routinely monitored and used to promote improvement. When that happens, a positive culture of evidence begins to take hold that is far easier to maintain than the sudden and difficult conversations that happen in response to disruptive events such as the pandemic. Over time, the culture will broaden to encompass areas such as strategic finance, enrollment, student success, research, scholarship, and creative activity.

Monitoring the Financial Health of Programs

The COVID-19 pandemic accelerated downward trends and introduced new challenges. Enrollments cratered and state budget deficits ballooned, and had it not been for federal stimulus funds, many colleges would have faced an existential crisis. Senior campus leaders were already concerned about precarious finances, but after the pandemic began, all levels of campus communities became painfully aware of the implications. New hires were frozen, faculty lines were retracted, massive numbers of adjunct faculty were not reappointed, collectively bargained raises were delayed, and budgets were cut across the board. These shocks have a way of raising institutional consciousness about money.

The metrics that provosts and deans use to measure financial health, such as the costs of instruction and advising, workloads, average teaching loads, class sizes, student-faculty ratios, and the ratio of tenure-track faculty to adjunct faculty, are useful at a high level, but they lose utility at the department chair level because a lot of variation exists across departments. Imagine trying to apply a standard student-faculty ratio across history, dance, nursing, and biology. Someone is going to feel like they are getting short shrift. Department chairs need financial measures that complement those provosts and deans use and offer them operational value. Table 6.2 describes some of those measures.

These metrics provide department chairs with actionable indicators that can maximize resources, spread work evenly among faculty, and determine if release time is being used appropriately and in pursuit of department, school, and college goals. The primary challenge related to teaching capacity and student credit hours is pulling data together from integrated systems, which usually is a manual job even though it is possible to automate it. For release time, the primary challenge is that the data do not usually exist in an organized way. The bigger and harder challenge to overcome, however, is that the provision of release time is often a political exercise. It often results from handshake agreements between a provost or dean and individual faculty members. Therefore, initial efforts to gather release time data can be met with resistance, especially if there are concerns that it might get clawed back or redistributed. The possibility of changes to release time is a powerful deterrent when the relationships between chairs and faculty are taken into consideration, but given that release time can equal 10-20% of a college's budget, few institutions can afford to misunderstand and misuse it.

Enrollment as a Signal of Program Health

The number of students within a given major is a rudimentary signal of a department's place in the pecking order and an indicator

TABLE 6.2. *Department chair cost metrics*

Measure	Calculation	Application
Teaching capacity differentials	Variation among faculty from average faculty teaching load	This measure helps department chairs understand whether they are offering an optimal number of courses, which has implications for hiring adjuncts. It can be used for creating the term schedule and managing faculty appointments.
Ratio of student credit hours taught to full-time faculty	Average credit hours per faculty full-time equivalent	This measure helps identify opportunities to balance low-enrollment courses with high-enrollment courses. When measures are calculated and applied to clusters of similar departments (e.g., experiential programs, large lecture programs), it can help make it possible to offer courses with diverse enrollments.
Release time analysis	Average course release time for faculty; evidence of productivity	This measure helps uncover patterns and trends in release time and its productivity. Often, faculty have received release time for things such as research, assessment, or service in ad hoc ways. This practice can lead to an unhealthy accumulation of release time that can have real implications for department budgets. In some instances, understanding the ratio of release time to scholarly productivity is easy to calculate, but in other instances, such as the quality of assessment, more qualitative data are needed to determine whether or not release time is being used effectively.

Source: EAB (Education Advisory Board), *Academic Vital Signs: Aligning Departmental Evaluation with Institutional Priorities* (Washington, DC: EAB, 2018).

of program health. The number of majors can be used as a means of soft influence since colleges and universities have become more dependent on enrollment revenue in recent decades. Given that enrollment at the college and department levels has become increasingly variable and hard to predict, raw major counts do not provide enough insight. A more nuanced way of thinking about enrollment and the important role that *all* programs, big and small, have to play in maintaining a healthy college is needed.

Departments play different and often complementary roles within an institution. Cutting-edge STEM majors and nursing schools attract students but are expensive to run. Humanities departments such as English, fine arts, and history may not make headlines but they are comparatively inexpensive to fund and provide most of an institution's general education core. When you consider the frequency with which students switch between colleges and majors, the need for solid academic and student supports for transitions, whether those take place between institutions within the same system or academic programs within the same college, are increasingly important for student success and for maintaining enrollment and academic momentum.

As the composition of student bodies have changed, so too have course-taking habits. The traditional focus on fall and spring enrollment does not tell the full story, and it may be disadvantaging students and colleges. For example, in the early 2010s many colleges adopted fifteen-to-finish efforts, which strongly encouraged students to take fifteen credits per semester based on the simple math that taking twelve credits each semester means that students will not graduate within four years.[5] Taking fewer credits each semester results in additional time to earn a degree, opens the possibility of accruing more debt, and puts students in the position of having to pay for more college instead of reaping the benefits of a postgraduate earnings bump. Over time, many colleges have realized that taking thirty credits per year is a better approach for their students, especially if those credits are stretched out through summer and winter terms. This strategy makes the department chair's task of scheduling courses increasingly important and more dynamic. Chairs need data so they can look ahead and ensure that the right courses and sections are available each term.

It is also important to realize that colleges and universities cannot disentangle academic programs from local and regional employment needs. Students want jobs when they graduate and employers want highly skilled and competent people to join their companies. Higher education is the traditional go-between, whether through credit-bearing or non-credit-bearing programs. Enrollment in a particular program can often depend on uncontrollable things rather than on intentional approaches to marketing and branding. Given that challenge, the metrics provided in table 6.3 can help department chairs get a better handle on enrollment so they can take actions that will promote growth.

These metrics and analyses can help department chairs identify patterns and trends in progression within the major, promote targeted variation in term-to-term scheduling, and recalibrate particular dimensions of the program in anticipation of the future needs of employers and likely student interests, all of which are important in promoting student success.

Student Success and Equity

Department chairs are as near the front lines of student success as you can get, and their position one level above individual faculty members gives them the potential to have a transformative impact on student success and equity. Yet doing so requires measures and metrics that may look slightly different from those with presidents, provosts, and deans are usually concerned with. For example, while a provost may want to see four-, five-, and six-year graduation rates by major, that information is of little use to a chair for two reasons. First, few students declare and are placed in a major the moment they arrive on campus as first-year stu-

TABLE 6.3. *Department chair enrollment metrics and applications*

Measure	Data source(s)	Application
Student registration metrics	Registration statistics; student hold information	Registration metrics help department chairs determine whether registration is progressing at levels higher or lower than previous years and if the pace of registration is faster or slower than usual. It can help identify barriers that get in the way of a student enrolling. Measures include the difference between the total number of registered students and those who are eligible, the average number of credits students have registered for, and the number of unregistered students with holds.
Major flows	Difference between students who have declared the major and those who are switching out	Major flows help determine if a program is experiencing net major growth or decline from term to term. It can signal whether barriers to enrollment exist within a specific program, such as difficult prerequisites, high GPA requirements, or exams. For example, a student could declare that a nursing major but switch to a different major if they fail to meet the minimum GPA requirement or entrance exam score.
Course efficiency metrics	Difference between total students enrolled and the maximum number possible	Class enrollment and capacity metrics help department chairs understand how demand for a particular course or sequence of courses has changed over time. They can help determine how frequently to offer a course and gauge the courses that are in highest and lowest demand. Courses with lower fill rates could be collapsed into fewer sections and courses with higher fill rates could benefit from having resources reallocated to them.

(continued)

TABLE 6.3. *(continued)*

Measure	Data source(s)	Application
Anticipated course demand	Prerequisite grade data and enrollment data	Because of the traditional two-semester model, colleges have grown accustomed to offering one slate of courses in the fall and one slate of courses in the spring with little difference from year to year. By identifying prerequisite courses and looking at the proportion of students who pass or pass with a minimum grade, chairs can schedule the next course in the sequence appropriately.
Special session enrollment	Demand for specific prerequisite and required courses	By analyzing student degree audits and reviewing anticipated course demand, chairs can schedule just-in-time courses during off-peak terms using multiple modalities. This strategy is increasingly important because of the changing nature of student enrollment, which often extends beyond the traditional two-semester format.
Net employer demand	Comparing employer demand with the supply of potential graduates	Understanding future employer needs using data from state agencies, the Bureau of Labor Statistics, or jobs data platforms helps chairs identify gaps in program offerings and opportunities to expand certain components of programs. If current enrollment and the expected number of graduates are below future occupational projections, the program may need to be adapted, expanded, and/or rebranded to become a more attractive destination for students.

Source: Education Advisory Board, *Academic Vital Signs: Aligning Departmental Evaluation with Institutional Priorities* (Washington, DC: EAB, 2018).

dents. Second, nearly 40% of all students transfer at least once, and there is wide variation in the number of credits they transfer between institutions, even though more campuses are working to create more seamless transfer experiences.[6] Since nearly every student has a different starting point within a major, metrics with a fixed starting point early in the academic journey of all students offer little value and may even be counterproductive.

The measures departments work with need to be related to things they can influence. If they have no control over metrics such as first-year-student retention rates or credit accrual rates or employment and earnings after graduation, they have no use for that data. What departments can influence are grades, time and credits to degree past a certain point (usually major declaration), student engagement and experiences, collaboration with career development specialists; and learning management system analytics.

Course grade analyses have usually focused on the proportion of course grades that are D, F, W (withdrawn) and sometimes D, F, W, and I (incomplete) in key courses such as important prerequisites, course sequences, general education or common core courses, and courses that are required for a student to be accepted into a major. One word of caution: while the focus on DFW grades is warranted, attention should also be paid to the proportion of A and B grades over time. They could suggest grade inflation, which is its own problem. When grade analyses are combined with course enrollment data, it becomes clear very quickly where there are opportunities to improve student outcomes and preserve academic quality. The example in table 6.4 clearly shows that there may be challenges related to the core math sequence, especially pre-calculus and calculus courses.

Taking a slightly different view of the math sequence in table 6.4 provides a little more information (see table 6.5). From college algebra to precalculus to calculus I, the average grade and number of students decreases, while the variation in grades goes up.

TABLE 6.4. *Math sequence analysis, academic year 2014–15 to academic year 2018–19 (hypothetical IR office data)*

Course name	Percent DFIW	Enrollment
Pre-Calculus	27.4	3,200
Calculus 1	44.8	2,200
General Physics 1	35.2	1,100
Politics and Culture	21.6	1,200
Calculus 2	31.0	1,100

Note: Includes the following grades: D+, D, F, I, W.

TABLE 6.5. *Average grades by course, math sequence (hypothetical IR office data)*

Course name	Average grade	Number students	Standard deviation
A1. Algebra and Numbers I	2.3	80	1.41
A2. College Algebra	2.9	2,630	1.37
C1. Elements of Pre-Calculus	3.0	80	1.16
C1B. Pre-Calculus	2.7	1,500	1.42
C2. Calculus I	2.3	915	1.59
C3. Calculus II	2.7	426	1.40

Chairs can take a deeper dive into individual course grade data to see if the variation indicates equity gaps. In table 6.6, the data shows that multiple equity gaps exist for women, for students of color, and for women of color. The department can explore different pedagogical approaches such as flipped classrooms; seek resources for tutoring and advising; strengthen assessment activity; and seek out philanthropic support to address these issues.

More Nuanced Persistence Metrics

Efforts to measure major graduation rates are ill advised for most college departments because few students declare a major as first-

TABLE 6.6. *Average calculus I course grades by student race/ethnicity (hypothetical IR office data)*

Race/ethnicity	Gender Female	Male	Total average
American Indian/Alaska Native	—[a]	—[a]	—[a]
Asian	2.5	2.3	2.4
Black	2.2	2.0	2.2[b]
Hispanic	2.3	2.0	2.2
Native Hawaiian/Other Pacific Islander	2.4	2.2	2.3
White	2.5	2.2	2.4[b]
More than one race	2.1	2.0	2.1
International students	2.1	2.0	2.1

[a] Cell size fewer than 10.

[b] Value rounded up.

year students, their journey to their final major is often circuitous, and transfer students bring varying levels of credits. Creating measures that reflect these realities are more useful for departments. Measures should take into consideration the fact that students declare their majors at different points in their academic careers and often have accumulated different numbers of credits by the time they declare. For example, the University of Maine evaluates academic departments based on graduation rates and time-to-degree metrics that are calculated once a student reaches junior status.[7] Departments that have low junior graduation rates must create plans to improve course grades, perhaps using the DWF model discussed above; refine transfer articulation and alignment; and strengthen student learning outcomes based on assessment and continuous improvement.

Adult and Continuing Education

Serving social and economic needs has always been a vital element of America's colleges and universities. US higher education history is replete with examples of innovations in the curriculum.[8] The industrial revolution gave rise to various technical colleges. Westward expansion and policy levers like the Morrill Act led to land-grant universities and agricultural programs. Social and economic shifts in the mid-twentieth century revealed the need for advances in technology, leading to programs related to computer science and specialized engineering programs. Ongoing efforts by colleges to evolve their academic programs in ways that align with social, political, and economic demands have inspired an increasing demand for a college education. In 2019, for the first time in US history, more than 50% of adults aged 25 to 34 had a college degree.[9] Despite this progress, there is a long way to go; recent data from the U.S. Department of Labor indicated that 90% of new jobs are going to people with a college degree.[10]

Higher education must once again readjust in the face of a transformation characterized by job automation, the emergence of the gig economy, and the changing nature of doing business. As jobs that require routinized labor dwindle, the demand for critical thinking, creativity, and skilled technical workers will continue to grow, as will employees' needs for lifelong learning, upskilling, and reskilling. To meet these needs, institutions will undoubtedly go through another era of curricular renewal. Perhaps as important, colleges will also need to revisit the structure and pacing of programs.

In addition to developing a strategic and coordinated approach to these activities, senior campus leaders will need to lead efforts to dispel the assumption that learning and working are mutually exclusive activities. To navigate this challenge, colleges and universities will need to develop metrics that promote the creation of new and restructured programs and that blend the worlds of credit- and non-credit-bearing programs. In this process, colleges can help students engage in lifelong learning in a more episodic way that is in keeping with the flexibility and convenience they need. In addition, colleges can encourage the periodic return of students who want to pursue additional stackable and linkable credentials. Relevant measures are included in table 6.7.

Done routinely and in partnership with local employers, evidence-based curricular reviews of adult and continuing education programs represent an opportunity for academic program renewal that can help programs and courses remain current, make graduates more attractive to employers, and enhance the reputation of the program. Now is the time to leverage data to improve their status and more fully integrate them into the institution.

Ensuring Quality Learning Regardless of Modality

Over the last few years, academic departments, particularly those that require face-to-face interaction, have made it a point to strengthen their remote teaching and learning as students acclimate to synchronous and asynchronous modalities. Because of this, a need has emerged to assess and reconfigure courses to make them equally effective regardless of modality and synchronicity. In turn, individual faculty members have had to refamiliarize themselves with their learning management system with a particular focus on usage data.

Tracking and comparing the amount of time that students spend in their online course shells relative to the total number of anticipated course minutes offers some value in determining the likelihood that a student will succeed or fail in a course. These data can inform how departments leverage their learning management system course shells and advising platforms to nudge students to log in and use available platforms. Some key indicators for student engagement include total number of logins, average minutes per student login, and days since the last login. It is important to review differences in course engagement across different student traits and the intersections of various traits.

Tracking faculty engagement with their learning management system course shells is equally important, including the total

TABLE 6.7. *Measures for adult and continuing education (ACE) (hypothetical IR office data)*

Measure	Notes
Employment rate for students who complete credential	Given that many ACE and noncredit programs are short cycle and focused on careers/vocations, measures of employment represent the only and ultimate payoff.
Income and percent income above local living wage standards	The credential should contribute to earnings value above what is considered a local living wage. If students with credentials continue to work in low-wage occupations without seeing some bump in pay relative to the per capita income or other comparable earnings benchmark, the program needs to be reviewed and reconfigured. Otherwise, the primary objective has not been accomplished.
Enrollment pathways from ACE to degree programs (includes percent students who start in ACE and then enter degree programs)	As enrollments become increasingly variable and harder to predict and the need for lifelong learning increases, creating bridges between credit-bearing and non-credit-bearing programs is a win-win for the student and the school. Quantifying the number of pathways and measuring their use adds value to academic programs because it creates more pipelines to longer-cycle credentials and to students who will need to engage and reengage episodically throughout life.
Percent of students who obtain credentials/licenses	For programs that have an exam or licensure requirement at the end, such as social work, knowing the percentage of students who become licensed is crucial. If they do not earn the credential or get a license, the student has lost both money and time, a major opportunity cost.
Percent of programs that are reviewed and validated by employers every 1–2 years	When employers are not engaged in curricular renewal, programs tend to atrophy, whether they are on the credit-bearing or non-credit-bearing side of the college. It is important to engage in meaningful and continuous refreshing of programs.

number of minutes they have accessed the course; the average amount of time they spent logged in; and the ratio of enrolled, active, and inactive students. Understanding differences in these metrics by academic rank, academic program, or any other college service that uses the learning management system is also important because it might reveal opportunities for the institution to provide targeted pedagogical or non-academic supports that lead to greater student engagement. Together, these data can help departments successfully shift from face-to-face to online instruction. This type of course delivery will become increasingly important to colleges over the next decade.

Research, Scholarship, and Creative Activity

Academic departments serve multiple purposes. While the most important function is serving students, the role that programs play in the creation of knowledge and creative works is a key driver of faculty success and satisfaction. Unfortunately, colleges and universities often do not prioritize research and creative activities when they are thinking about creating a comprehensive data system. How departments measure success in this area can vary, depending on how mature the research infrastructure is at an institution. An institution focused on teaching rather than on major research activity might focus on quantity if it intends to grow its research portfolio, while an institution with a larger and established research profile p might focus on quality. Table 6.8 offers a series of metrics to consider and some context about how institutions with different degrees of research intensiveness might prioritize them. Departments that want to determine which research and innovation measures to focus on will need a robust office of research to support the work and codify the standards and policies that promote a strategic and sustainable research infrastructure.

Clear standards and measures for assessing resource allocation help departments expand their research portfolios. A strategic

TABLE 6.8. *Types of research and innovation metrics and how colleges prioritize them based on maturity of research infrastructure*

Metric category	Research infrastructure status		
	Immature	Emerging	Mature
Broader college investment in research infrastructure	L	M	H
Number of research grant proposals	H	M	L
Size of potential grant	L	M	H
Success rate of grant proposals	L	M	H
Proportion of faculty applying for grants	L	M	H
Alignment of grants to department priorities	L	M	H
Individual faculty proposals	H	M	L
Transdisciplinary proposals	L	M	H
Grants with an indirect cost recovery rate of <10%	H	M	L
Grants with an indirect cost recovery rate of >10% and <20%	M	H	M
Grants with an indirect cost recovery rate of >20%	L	M	H
Number of creative works	M	M	H
Return on investment of release time	L	M	H
Patent and copyright activity	L	M	H
Number of articles published	H	M	M
Quality of articles published	M	H	H
Cross-sector partnerships	M	H	H

Note: L = lowest, M = medium, H = highest.

goal set by the provost to increase research and scholarly and creative activity can have unintended consequences unless parameters regarding the size of grants pursued and the indirect cost recovery rate are clearly defined in collaboration with scholars and researchers. If grants are not large enough and if indirect costs are not appropriately identified, individual faculty members will earn grants without allocating resources for important support services like assessment, evaluation, institutional research, administration, and facilities. At colleges that have been resourced to build out the infrastructure to support and invest in research and creative activities, established metrics and policies related to these areas help ensure that these support services are appropriately funded and staffed. These policies and procedures translate into better evaluation of grants, less stress on data capacity, and a more intentional approach that leads to continued improvement in both the quality and funding of research grants.

Conclusion

Institutional effectiveness depends on the quality of academic programs, yet communication and relationships sometimes break down between departments and presidents, provosts, and deans because of perspectives that are in tension with one another. Senior campus leaders sometimes mistakenly believe that the measures they use to monitor and improve the performance of the entire college are equally applicable to the front line, which is usually occupied by the department chair. Chairs hold the keys to a unique economy of scale that usually tells the story of whether a college is successfully pursuing its goals. To unlock the collective impact of departments, an institution's staff and faculty need to commit to using timely, accurate, relevant, and integrated data in actionable ways.

Chapter 7

Creating a Data
Governance System

In the past, many in academe have viewed data governance as a relatively static construct: a data set with a lot of information that few people take the time to explore. The stable nature of data governance fit well with the strategic and operational nature of colleges and universities during normal times, but we are living in anything but normal times. Converging pressures, the evolving nature of student bodies, and the effects of the pandemic have revealed that traditional data governance is no longer optimal. A unique opportunity to retune data governance into something more fluid, engaging, and inclusive has emerged as a result. Senior campus leaders who seize the moment can use data governance to develop stronger, more sustainable cultures of evidence. Fueled by the widespread adoption of a federated model of informed data users and by using artificial intelligence and machine learning to sift through tremendous amounts of data, colleges and universities can become more dynamic and resilient organizations.

The evolution of leadership is converging with new approaches to handling data at just the right time.

The opportunity to reimagine data governance has emerged in response to growing demands for data and analytics that produce meaningful insights quickly and reliably. This is because, as the old saying goes, "garbage in, garbage out." Good governance helps ensure that the data created and the analyses conducted lead to trustworthy and meaningful findings. As demands for more and increasingly varied forms of data have increased, data governance has grown in importance. These demands span a number of traditional areas, such as student success, equity, academic planning, and strategic finance. New topics have surfaced in response to student needs and environmental conditions, such as student mental health and well-being, device and internet access, housing and food insecurity, and deep learning analytics, as noted in chapter 2. Within and across these topics, the volume and variety of available data have exploded. Only recently have some colleges and universities successfully developed the capabilities to collect, process, connect, and study big data in its many forms and use it to understand and enhance the student experience in highly personalized and potentially transformative ways. To institutionalize these capacities, college and university leaders have to get serious about data governance and utility.

What Is Data Governance?

If the world's most valuable resource is now data, as *The Economist* stated in 2017, it is vitally important to preserve it and maximize its value.[1] Data governance helps in this process, and new definitions are helping campus leaders generate greater interest in sustained engagement on the matter. Recently, the National Association of College and University Budget Officers defined data governance as "an institution's data strategy that outlines rights and responsibilities for how stakeholders across campus can manage and use data."[2] Rana Glasgal and Valentina Nestor argue that good data governance should anticipate opportunities and challenges related to data and should be widespread across the organization. They define it as "a multi-functional organizational strategic initiative which enables, enforces, and formalizes the proactive management of its essential data assets to achieve the organization's business goals."[3] In other words, institutions should use data governance to continuously manage and use data and analytics in ways that facilitate progress toward or achievement of college goals.

The consensus among emerging definitions of data governance is that data governance refers to how colleges and universities make sense of their data and how the parameters that provide guidance about how to conduct analyses help ensure that data are high quality, broadly understood, and secure, among other things. Data governance is the foundation upon which sound analyses are built. Without it, the quality of an institution's data is likely to be poor. That is bad for senior campus leaders, and yet it is where many find themselves. It takes more than good data to change that, however. The trick is getting people to use data.

Modern definitions of data governance have evolved to focus on the use of data in pursuit of strategic objectives. This subtle extension of the definition is important because it emphasizes maximizing the value of an organization's data instead of just stewarding and protecting it. Of course, building and maintaining a modern approach to data governance and utility is a complex undertaking that should only be embarked upon if the will and the resources exist to take on the heavy lift and sustain it as a strategic organizational priority. It takes commitment.

Colleges and universities have different starting points related to data governance. A well-established data governance framework helps create data-enabled leaders who "look around the corner" on behalf of their college or university by making sense of a lot of data in timely, accurate, relevant, and integrated ways that are reflective, predictive, and prescriptive. Few colleges and universities have fully mature data governance capabilities, however. There is no shame in that, especially given that it is difficult to mobilize a campus to accept data analytics. That is because that shift can lead to organizational changes that are often unwelcome even when they are healthy and overdue. Table 7.1 illustrates the stages of developing a data governance system. Very few colleges and universities have reached the point where their data governance efforts are sustained and self-renewing because of common challenges that are difficult to overcome.

College and university leaders who have already taken steps to ensure the quality of data and to safeguard it have created a solid foundation for building a culture of evidence. But data needs to be used in ways that generate insights and lead to actions that benefit students and contribute to a more sustainable campus. Unfortunately, the spaces that are usually asked to generate those insights and make recommendations, such as offices of institutional research and/or institutional effectiveness and a growing number of new officers and roles focused on strategy, policy, and analytics lack sufficient people power to keep up with a list of requests that continues to grow.

Most colleges and universities lack deep pockets to invest in positioning themselves at the cutting edge of artificial intelligence and machine learning. Instead, they operate more like small businesses. They need to rely on scaling out the strategic use of data by investing resources in training and professional development for everyone, from advisors to faculty to cabinet members. Without ensuring that people have the skills and expertise needed to use data routinely and effectively, efforts to create a culture of evidence will fail.

Structural, technical, organizational, political, and personal dynamics all contribute to the uneven distribution and use of higher education data. As a result, very few people at a particular campus have a 360-degree, data-informed view of what is working and what needs fixing. The absence of a comprehensive view during exceptionally volatile times is a major vulnerability.

TABLE 7.1. *Stages in developing a mature data governance system*

Initial	A formal vision for strategic data use does not exist. There is no data governance and utility committee. Data and processes are highly siloed, uneven, and often unknown. Trust in institutional data is nonexistent. Data are not used. There are no champions
Emergent	A formal vision for strategic data use does not exist. There is no data governance utility committee. Data and processes are mostly siloed, although a few exceptions exist in core data buckets. Trust in institutional data is uneven. Data are not widely used. There are few informal champions.
Structured	A formal vision for strategic data use is being created. A data governance and utility committee has been established. Some data and processes are automated and integrated but are not yet scaled out. Trust in data is growing. Access to data has not yet been scaled out. Champions are emerging.
Integrated	A formal vision for strategic data use has been created. A data governance and utility committee has been established. Most data and processes are automated, integrated, and scaled out. Trust in data is high and access has begun to scale out to a critical mass. A few champions exist.
Applied	A formal vision for strategic data use has been created and is broadly understood. A data governance and utility committee has been established and is able to respond to opportunities and challenges in real time. Most processes and data have been highly integrated, automated, and scaled up. Trust in data is high. Access to data has been scaled out across the campus. Champions exist across the organization.
Sustained	A formal vision for strategic data use has been created, is broadly understood, and continuously guides campus strategies. A data governance and utility committee proactively identifies solutions to emerging opportunities and challenges related to data. All processes have been highly integrated, automated, and scaled out. Trust, access, and use of data are high throughout the campus and data are used in reflective, real-time, predictive, and prescriptive ways. Champions exist across the organization and effective and innovative data use is celebrated and rewarded in order to facilitate renewal.

Data governance can help senior campus leaders sharpen their vision if they properly structure, resource, socialize, celebrate, and commit to it.

Common Challenges

The launch of a data governance system can become bogged down for a number of reasons. Some leaders might be data skeptics or object to switching to a data analytics platform. The voluminous data a campus owns might be uneven and disconnected. Some people might be concerned about the risks associated with data privacy and information security. The campus might not have a strong culture of evidence that includes well-established, structures and rules for handling data well. The launch might not include enough investment in training people. The leaders promoting the launch might not have gone through the necessary steps to establish processes, policies, and technologies that facilitate the development of a culture of evidence and data use throughout the institution. The following paragraphs describe these challenges in more detail.

Barriers for Leaders

Most college and university leaders are not trained data scientists. They do not spend their days pondering the design flaws of their college's data infrastructure, crunching datasets, or creating algorithms—nor should they. The longer someone serves as a president, provost, or other senior campus leader, the farther away they are from spending time in a lab studying advanced statistical techniques or doing fieldwork. This distance can lead senior leaders to take a reductionist approach to the use of big data and analytics. They may focus on finding a pattern, pointing it out, and doing something about it—unless of course, the data are of uneven quality, in which case, things become complicated very quickly. If that situation is not resolved, it can create organizational paralysis.

Another challenge that stands in the way of a successful culture of evidence, of which data governance is a crucial component, is the realization that data can be untrustworthy. This can trigger apprehension among senior leaders, who have a reputation for relying on lived experience rather than facts and figures to make decisions, especially if the data are of dubious origin. If senior leaders are unwilling to adopt and stick to a data-informed approach, the campus will likely follow suit. The lack of adoption at the top is a poison pill, and the shrinking duration of presidential tenures disincentivizes leaders to play the long game and build a strong culture of evidence.

The Universe of Data Is Unwieldy, Unknown, and Unaccounted For

It is important to remember that data come from a variety of sources, such as an institution's enterprise resource planning system, learning management system, library system, customer relationship management system, content management system, registration system, and human resources system. While this is certainly not an exhaustive list, these major sources of campus data fall into a few general buckets that tend to be highly siloed and difficult to connect.

Colleges and universities get their data from hundreds of poorly connected places, both old and new (e.g., predictive analytics platforms, software applications, mobile devices, and campus Wi-Fi networks). These shadow systems usually develop because of bad data governance and are often embodiments of institutional tension and breakdowns in process and technology. Their existence illustrates how daunting the task of building and sustaining successful data governance can be. Take the example from Queens College in figure 7.1, which provides an image of what college data flows can look like. This illustration only begins

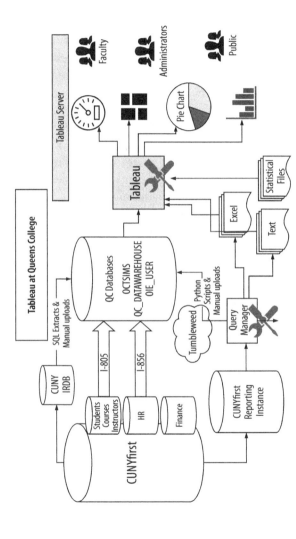

Figure 7.1. Queens College (City University of New York) data ecosystem

to scratch the surface of all the data sources that exist across a campus, many of which are unknown (e.g., shadow systems) and disconnected.

This disconnectedness stems from aging systems, poorly timed and poorly coordinated updates and upgrades, uneven communications across business units, a lack of resources and investment, and spotty commitment. Colleges are highly decentralized and often develop pockets of isolation based on organizational function and academic affiliation. The disintegrated nature of college and university data is rarely the result of an nefarious effort to intentionally undermine the institution. The truth is that the people who are charged with rolling up their sleeves and doing the work of a campus can become highly immersed in the operational components of their day-to-day labors because they care about students and believe in their institution. A map of the universe of data, as illustrated by figure 7.1, is an important component of drawing a complete picture for staff who can benefit from using data from different sources. The universe of data is in a constant state of flux, so the map needs to be tended and shared continuously.

Information Privacy and Security Is Complex and Current Policies Are Insufficient

The internal and external systems that produce and share data creates introduce privacy and security risks. These hazards are intensifying given the proliferation of biometric data (e.g., facial and speech data) that hackers can use to access bank records, cell phone data, and internet browsing activity. In 2020, the worst year on record so far, there were 3,932 publicly reported data breaches that exposed more than 37 billion records.[4] The education sector was breached 223 times that year. Misconfigured databases and services were the leading reason that records were exposed.

Industry researchers have also cited internal threats, whether intentional or accidental, as major threats to information privacy and security. Some of these threats are caused by lax computer use (such as employees sharing login information or clicking on unknown links from external sources) and outdated information technology policies can leave campuses highly vulnerable to breaches caused by hacking, social attacks, malware, and misuse by employees.[5] Given that stiff penalties accompany new policies—such as the European General Data Protection Regulation, which many consider to be the toughest privacy and security law in the world, or the California Consumer Privacy Act—senior campus leaders must modify data privacy and information security policies to ensure that data breaches do not occur. Updating computer technology is another key element of data security.

In efforts to create policies around data governance and use, including privacy and security protocols, great care should be taken to avoid some of the issues that arise when more stringent policies are put in place. Examples include greater difficulty accessing data in a timely fashion or a feeling on the part of some campus stakeholders that data policies threaten their academic freedom. When such issues emerge, campus members could respond by creating shadow data systems that cancel the benefits of comprehensive privacy and information security policies.

Campus Culture and Structures Are Not Properly Focused on Data Governance

Too often, data governance is left to chief information officers and institutional research directors. Even under optimal circumstances, where a strong and collaborative relationship exists between these two groups, data governance is hard work. Unfortunately, the relationship between an office of information technology and institutional research is often complicated.

Conflicts over finite resources; ownership of data strategy, where there is one; and turf battles stifle collaboration. Both divisions usually have conservative dispositions toward granting access to data, albeit for different reasons. Information technology has valid concerns about privacy and security, whereas institutional research dreads having to provide multiple answers to common questions from local data enthusiasts who lack context. The shared tendency of a campus's two biggest data gatekeepers to build walls around data sources can run counter to modern approaches to data governance that focus on getting integrated data into the hands of people at scale. The degree to which these divisions can work together to resolve this conflict in approaches to data is the focus of a much larger national discussion about the future of institutional research and institutional technology. Getting institutional research and institutional technology staff on board with a plan to move toward integrated data analytics is key. If those two departments can collaborate in their support of that effort, it will go a long way toward determining the success of a president or provost who is leading the process.

The Campus Is Not Engaged in the Conversation around Data Governance

It takes a village to do data governance well, especially given the uneven and disconnected state of a growing array of institutional data. Many campuses, however, lack a representative body that works toward creating and integrating better data for broad campus use through the implementation of an intentional strategy. Academic affairs, student affairs, accounts and billing, financial services, human resources, school deans, department chairs, and especially faculty and students need to be engaged. They all either have or are the embodiment of campus data and have unique perspectives that humanize data governance efforts. However, the perspectives of these units are rarely brought together in their totality in conversations about data governance.

People Distrust the Launch of Data Governance Efforts

Initially, a big-tent approach to data governance and utility can be a hard sell. It requires that people let down their guard, establish trust, and share data. The siloed nature of data ownership is a barrier to an integrated approach to data governance that is cultural and technical. Many campus stakeholders work hard to preserve territory and feel that keeping their data separate from an integrated system is important. Data integration can also lead to corrosion of a unified campus culture when people believe that data will be used punitively, not positively, and that any effort by campus administration to get their hands on data is a veiled effort to create efficiencies, slash budgets, and rationalize the reduction of programs or jobs in dire financial times.

It would be easy to dismiss common anxieties about data governance as a natural state, but it would be wrong to do so. Establishing a strong data governance system is such a fraught undertaking because it tends to be neglected until there is a crisis, and a crisis often leaves a negative imprint because some drastic action winds up being taken. The repetitive association of negative experiences with data governance efforts are what make them such a tough sell. That is why data governance must be consistently attended to in a positive way. It is important to create and sustain dedicated routines and platforms for an ongoing discussion about effective data governance and use. These might take the form of a weekly meeting, an asynchronous discussion board, or an annual celebration of good data governance that highlights a collaborative approach between various institutional departments. This is an intense effort, so dedicated personnel need to be committed to driving engagement, creating accountability mechanisms, and providing incentives to participate in an integrated data system.

Launching and Sustaining Successful Data Governance Efforts

To harness the immense potential of big data and the analytics revolution, college and university executives need to develop a comprehensive data strategy that emphasizes data governance. Yet doing so is more valuable and difficult than ever. Demands for data and the insights they can provide have increased exponentially even though the ability of people, processes, policies, and technologies to meet them has not kept pace. As a result, college leaders must adopt innovative approaches to data governance.

Lead with Vision and Intentionality

The first step in starting a robust data governance program is creating a vision and setting clear expectations about who will use the data and to what ends. This involves creating a clear set of goals that help clarify the strategic direction and priorities of the campus, which should ultimately shape the scope of a data strategy. When José Luis Cruz, former president of Lehman College, launched the 90 x 30 Challenge mentioned in chapter 3, he built an evidence-based, equity-driven program on a foundation of data and technology. 90 x 30 painted a picture of a more impactful future if the campus could organize, improve, and integrate its data in support of greater educational attainment in the Bronx. Creating a clear vision, communicating it frequently across the campus, and embedding the importance of data and analytics into the aspiration helped elevate awareness of the future importance of data.

Launching a data governance program involves creating a campus engagement plan that clearly articulates the institution's data strategy and says how it will be used to steer the organization. It is also important to set expectations about creating a culture of evidence and developing standards that ensure that data are up to date, accurate, relevant, integrated, and accessible.

As part of its famous data-informed transformation, Georgia State University (GSU) did just that. As Timothy Renick notes, "GSU's President Mark Becker drew a line in the sand by announcing [that] at university meetings and for university decision-making (such as budgeting) he would only consider data that was housed in the university's central data system."[6] Becker knew that using data-based evidence in strategic visioning exercises and when making major decisions would help deconstruct silos and accelerate the sharing and integration of data.

By regarding data as a university-wide asset, leaders at GSU began to shift how people viewed data. Instead of seeing data as a widely dispersed, decentralized asset, campus stakeholders began to see it as something the entire university owned and could use and was responsible for stewarding. This change in attitude cleared the way for better data integration and a clearer view of where integration could be improved in support of GSU's strategic goals.

Design a Data Governance Process

When senior campus leaders articulate a clear data strategy that supports institutional goals, they create an opportunity to assess just how ready the campus is to use data effectively. This is also the time to organize data sources and governance standards and practices. At the University of North Texas (UNT), this exercise took the form of Insights 2.0, a collaborative effort among "Data, Analytics, and Institutional Research (DAIR), Analytic Information Solutions (AIS) in Finance and Administration, and ITSS team members from UNT System" that built the structures, tools, and processes the university needed to ensure that sound data are at the core of effective decision-making. UNT used a comprehensive approach to taking inventory of campus data and analyzing how it was gathered, defined, and used. This assessment was developed in support of UNT's commitment to a data governance process, which was built on two guiding principles. First, no dashboards would be published without being fully documented and vetted by DAIR. Second, campus data would be presented in its source (original) form. To achieve these goals in an open and transparent way, Insights 2.0 created a network of technical, functional, and subject matter experts to make data governance a shared and ongoing responsibility.[7]

Create and Empower a Data Governance Committee

When the University of Maryland, Baltimore County (UMBC) began its data governance effort, senior campus leaders knew that success would require a big-tent strategy. At first, stakeholders responded to the initial decision to centralize and standardize the university's approach to data governance with concerns that other groups would have access to their data. To overcome these initial concerns, a data management committee was created with representatives from each UMBC college and administrative division. The committee, which met each semester, focused on providing guidance and oversight. Several subcommittees were also created to focus on the issues of warehousing, user groups, data quality, data access and security, and training. These subcommittees were composed of a collaborative group of stakeholders that included representatives from institutional research, finance and administration, information technology, and a constellation of academic, administrative, and technical subject matter experts.[8]

That is how UMBC convinced stakeholders of the importance of an ongoing approach to data governance. Given the growing volume of increasingly diverse data, constant attention to how data is handled is vitally important. Moreover, given the potential for implicit bias in how data is created, collected, and analyzed, any data governance committee should be charged with reviewing data and analytics tools for potential biases that could lead to inequitable provision of academic and student supports. This activity is especially important given the emergence of predictive analytics and the use of artificial intelligence and machine learning on academic campuses (see chapter 8).

Get Champions and Celebrate Successes

Developing a coalition of data governance champions is an important element of sustaining data governance efforts. Initial progress can be difficult to see unless the campus community knows where to look. To help the campus to recognize success, senior leaders should ensure that data governance committee members are visible and enthusiastic champions of improving and facilitating the use of data. It takes a special person to serve in that role well, and it is important to identify champions across all levels of the institution—from senior administrators to members of faculty and student governing bodies to members of the cabinet and the board. Choosing the right people to serve as leaders in creating a strong data governance platform requires thoughtfulness and looking beyond job titles. It also involves developing a plan for identifying and communicating data governance achievements, both large and small. Creating a platform for broadcasting those accomplishments and identifying what rewards and incentives will be meaningful for those who take the lead can help frame data governance as a positive experience despite the negative beliefs campus stakeholders may have.

Develop a Measurement Framework for Success

Data governance requires a measurement framework. It is essential to identify key performance indicators and creating cycles of assessment and refinement. These indicators should be both quantitative and qualitative and should reflect the dual nature of the cultural and operational requirements of successful data governance. Metrics related to people are often a good place to start. The number of data owners, data sources, and data domains; the number of people who over time have engaged in the data governance program; and the time and resources spent diagnosing and anticipating challenges and opportunities are important indicators of data governance success. Tallying the number of training and professional development opportunities is also key. Better yet, if a certification program has been established, track the number of faculty and staff who are certified in the campus data governance program. Liz Henderson has highlighted numerous key performance indicators across a variety of dimensions.[9]

It is important to note the time, effort, and energy spent on refining how the college handles and uses data. Metrics can range from the creation and adoption of data governance policies to the number of requests that have been addressed and successfully completed. The number and usage rate of data products, such as dashboards and reports, can indicate the scale of the impact of data governance. Measuring the time it takes to create comparable products, such as analyses or dashboards, can help identify whether data governance is becoming more efficient and effective. Qualitative data, including satisfaction rates, satisfaction with campus engagements, and trust in the comprehensiveness and accessibility of data products, help maintain focus on the uses, quality, and scalability of data governance.

Understanding the impact of technological advancements enables senior campus leaders to develop a more complete record of the integrated nature of data. Measures related to the number of integrated data sources, the presence of shadow systems as a proportion of campus data, the modernization of a data dictionary, and the automation of data collection and product creation can help determine the breadth and depth of data governance and data use. Measures related to the accuracy and reliability of insight products keep senior campus leaders focused on getting data into the hands of campus stakeholders in timely, accurate, and relevant ways. When qualitative data from surveys and focus groups is routinely collected, it helps campus leaders identify trends and monitor the health and sustainability of an institution-wide culture of evidence.

Conclusion

Given the disruptive pressures facing higher education, colleges and universities need all personnel to have reliable access to quality data. This need became even more urgent during the pandemic, when faculty and staff engaged with students and each other remotely and more asynchronously than ever before. Effective approaches to data governance are vital to making sure that data are timely, accurate, relevant, integrated, and accessible to campus stakeholders. When data governance is done well, the result is better decision-making across all levels of the institution that leads to improved teaching, learning, and advising; better student outcomes; and optimization of campus resources. Successful data governance regimes involve careful planning; effective design and implementation; clarity about process; language, structures, platforms, and tools that ensure contextualized access; and forums for discussion and knowledge sharing. Data governance is an ongoing process that requires the commitment of the entire campus.

College executives have an important role to play in creating a positive climate for addressing data governance in ways that honor the campus and focus on student success and equity in a sustainable fashion. A commitment to data governance will increase the changes that a campus will succeed in an increasingly volatile environment. It will also lay the foundation upon which more advanced analytics capabilities can be built in ways that are responsible and ethical and that minimize the chances of misuse.

Chapter 8

The Promise and Peril of Data and Analytics

Inequity and bias are significant issues in higher education. Access to certain kinds of colleges and modalities is uneven. Gaps in retention, persistence, and completion have proven difficult to close. Curricula are often not diverse or representative. Senior campus leaders have wrestled with how to overcome structural issues on campus that reflect those of broader society. Many have gone to great lengths to better understand and organize data with the goal of eliminating inequities.

Recent success stories from campuses across the country have shown just how powerful predictive analytics, machine learning and artificial intelligence, and deep learning analytics can be in advancing those pursuits. However, senior campus leaders would be wise not to regard these tools as magical solutions. Just because a campus possesses the means to use advanced analytics does not mean that they are being used in a way that will decrease inequities. Irresponsible use could mean reinforcing systemic obstacles and biases instead of deconstructing them. Using data analytics is a simultaneously promising and perilous endeavor.

Big Data, Big Potential

The good news is that colleges and universities have a road map for successful use of advanced analytics. For example, predictive analytics and machine learning are helping administrators reimagine admissions by predicting which applicants are most likely to enroll, persist, and graduate. These data can highlight inequality and hindrances to upward mobility.[1] In 2019, the *Washington Post* recently reported that at least thirty-three colleges were using software to monitor and track the web browsing history of high school students, including social media data, to better estimate the likelihood that a student would enroll in their school if they were accepted.[2]

The proliferation of types of data—including biometric data, personal financial information, and social media information—has created new sources of information that institutions are using to profile students. The concern with this practice is that schools may be doing so with organizational goals in mind instead of prioritizing students' needs. Students have expressed apprehension about the use of their personal data, which they rightfully view as theirs to control. Students want to know how their data could be used and to decide if and how that will be allowed. They want colleges to use it in open and transparent ways that increase the likelihood that they will earn a degree.[3] This situation will only become more complicated as the analytics revolution continues to offer colleges more data that they can use either to surveil students or to facilitate their success.

Machine learning models can reveal opportunities to move admissions criteria away from standardized test scores and toward better indicators such as high school GPAs and course grades. Many campuses have improved their ability to sift through course-level high school transcript data. By identifying pockets of students who historically would not have been considered for admission but who are equally capable of earning a degree, colleges are broadening access, preserving academic momentum, and insulating themselves against competition by admitting students other institutions either have yet to identify or would turn away.[4]

Academic momentum and student outcomes have also benefited from the innovative use of advanced analytics. In the fall of 2016, Ivy Tech Community College, Indiana's community college system, used machine learning to reduce course failure rates by 3.3 percentage points, which was equivalent to 3,100 more students passing their classes compared to the previous year. Ivy Tech's information technology division worked collaboratively with academic affairs and student success staff to identify common characteristics of strong students and offer advice they would give to students who did not have those traits. The division then integrated data points that correlated with the advice that would be given into their analytical models.[5]

Cross-institutional partnerships strengthen college and university efforts to adopt predictive analytics and machine learning. For example, the Central Florida Education Ecosystem Database (CFEED) has brought four large-scale education institutions—Orange County Public Schools, the School District of Osceola County, the University of Central Florida (UCF), and Valencia College—into a single data repository. The consortium approach to data analytics has resulted in the use of machine learning techniques to improve the K-16 pipeline, accelerate college readiness, expand dual enrollment, improve math pathways, reduce transfer shock, and identify risk indicators. Valencia College and UCF have used historical data in CFEED to identify patterns in course completion. Armed with that knowledge, they calculated the probability of whether a student will stay in a major based on past and current course success. These analyses led to the development of targeted interventions designed to increase persistence.[6]

Using academic success, financial stability, belonging and engagement, and emotional and physical wellness as key indicators of student success, the University of Kentucky has implemented a values-focused approach to analytics. Weekly meetings attended by senior leadership, advisers, associate deans, enrollment management, and student services staff begin with a review of actionable business intelligence, which includes identifying "opportunity students" using a predictive model. These efforts are supported and led by Institutional Research, Analytics, and Decision Support, which uses predictive analytics to understand which variables affect retention in order to strengthen the effectiveness of micro-grants. The result has been substantial gains in second fall retention.[7] Despite these examples, higher education has only scratched the surface in its use of advanced analytics. The sector has only begun its journey.

The Cost of Misusing Data

Colleges can also use analytics in hazardous ways. Some of these dangers are obvious. For example, in 2015, Simon Newman, president of Mount St. Mary's University, developed a plan to "cull the class" of first-year students before September 25, a significant date because the federal government would consider the enrollment figure that day to be the official number used to calculate the university's retention rate. Newman calculated that by getting select students to leave, the retention rate would increase between 4 and 5%.[8]

In support of this goal, the Office of the President directed instructors to administer a survey that the administration hoped would "help us to develop better advanced metrics for accepting students."[9] In the weeks that followed, Newman instructed faculty to compile a list of students they deemed unlikely to complete their first year. When faculty and staff expressed concerns that this activity was unethical, the president remarked, "This is hard for you because you think of the students as cuddly bunnies, but you can't. You just have to drown the bunnies . . . put a Glock to their heads."[10] This statement created an uproar across the university and led to widespread calls for Newman's resignation. Initially, he vowed to continue in his role, but he eventually gave in to pressure and resigned on February 29, 2016.

This is a clear demonstration of a university president's intentional misuse of data and analytics. This type of misuse is so blatant that it usually generates strong, vocal, and consequential resistance. The real danger lies in the inadvertent ways that data can be misused and abused. As Manuela Ekowo and Iris Palmer have pointed out, many invisible risks are associated with the use of advanced analytics techniques, often stemming from bias in data that leads to discriminatory results, unfair labeling of students as deficient and at risk, and the perpetuation of the systemic inequities and human bias that permeate the fabric of society.[11] Issues related to accuracy, security, privacy data, and bias in AI and machine learning can introduce inequities in data and analytics that play out in the real world with devastating effects.[12]

Colleges and universities are highly vulnerable to these invisible risks because many of them are just beginning to understand the advantages and disadvantages of using analytics in modern ways. While pressure mounts for senior campus leaders to use these tools, too few have educated themselves about the risks and created policies to decrease them.

Learn from Others

Higher education can learn from the missteps of other sectors. The US health care system has been compared to higher education for decades because the two sectors have similar traits and challenges. The health care sector is increasingly using predictive analytics to identify patient needs. However, its broad adoption of algorithms to promote better, more efficient, and personalized care has been shown to be misdirected. Instead of using data to practice preventive health care, the sector has used it to predict health care costs. This misguided strategy has resulted in significant bias that has contributed to disproportionate rates of ineffective treatment for Black patients.[13]

Similar phenomena have been observed in the use of analytics to create job search ads, which tend to privilege men over women. Credit-market algorithms may promote bias, even when they are designed to do the very opposite.[14] Algorithms that process names and images, recognize faces, and process language have been shown to discriminate based on race and gender and the intersectionality of those characteristics.[15] In recent years, the use of facial recognition data has resulted in the misidentification of suspects, resulting in wrongful accusations of crime "based on erroneous but confident misidentification."[16] The improper and uninformed use of these kinds of data and analytics is dangerous. It is important for campus leaders to know where things can go wrong before they adopt data analytics on a large scale.

Be Vigilant against Bias

The root causes of the challenges that stem from data and analytics emerge from many places. It is important to remember that the systems and advanced analytics used to generate insights are only as comprehensive as their inputs, which include data, the process for creating and collecting data, and the people who analyze data. Unfortunately, data can be biased in different ways, including sample bias, confirmation bias, chronological bias, measurement bias, Simpson's paradox, overfitting or underfitting, correlation bias, stereotyping bias, and modeling bias.[17] The myriad forms of bias can "creep in during all phases of a project"[18] and are commonly found in data, in algorithms, and, most perniciously, in people.[19]

Nicol Turner Lee, Paul Resnick, and Genie Barton have highlighted how the mass scale of big data and analytics adoption can amplify human bias. They note that "bias in algorithms can emanate from unrepresentative or incomplete training data or the reliance on flawed information that reflects historical inequalities" and add that "if left unchecked, biased algorithms can lead to decisions which can have a collective, disparate impact on certain groups of people even without the programmer's intention to discriminate."[20] If there is sampling bias and data do not accurately reflect the population to which results will be generalized, analytics can magnify the bias.[21] For example, LinkedIn's search feature asks users who search for a female contact if instead they meant to search for a similarly spelled male name, but not the other way around. This happened because the model that powers the search feature relies heavily on frequency counts of names and males are more likely to have common names than females.[22] Alternatively, if data for a study are collected in such a way that some members of the sample are less likely to be included in the result, that creates ascertainment bias. A study that examined rates of Alzheimer's disease found that they were lower among statin users. However, those findings were called into question because a diagnosis requires a trip to the doctor, which is something that statin use may also be associated with.[23] Measurement error, or the presence of variables in a data set with inaccurately recorded values, can amplify differences between the reported value and the real value.[24] For example, biases in self-reported height and weight measurements such as height, weight, and body mass index can have effects on the modeling of health outcomes.[25] In each of these cases, the presence of different forms of bias in the data can be amplified by the emergence of big data and the analytics revolution.

Deeply held prejudices against certain groups can be magnified in computer algorithms. Such was the case when the Correctional Offender Management Profiling for Alternative Sanctions algorithm was found to judge incorrectly that Black defendants were more likely than white defendants to have a higher risk of recidivism.[26] The designers of the algorithm failed to identify and eliminate negative feedback loops that can contribute to the development of models that become more biased with more time and data.

The data used in predictive models often fall short of a representative sample, which also introduces bias. When the data fed into models are insufficiently representative of diverse citizens, patients, or students, the models tend to predict outcomes less reliably. A lack of diversity in among mathematicians, statisticians, and programmers who design and execute advanced models can find its way into analyses.[27] Imagine a college that has acquired an out-of-the-box predictive analytics solution. If the data used in the solution overrepresent or underrepresent students based on their traits (e.g., race/ethnicity, income, gender) and the people responsible for running the analyses and interpreting the findings are not diverse and lack information about the specific context of the college, the data may be biased and the analyses that are produced may not reflect the needs of underrepresented populations or the campus. Without ongoing care, these analyses and interventions can become increasingly skewed away from students of color and first-generation and low-income students, further disadvantaging those who already often struggle in an unfair system. The same challenges may emerge for part-time students, working learners, and students who are parents or caregivers. All of these groups constitute a growing share of the undergraduate student body, but their experiences and needs may not be reflected in data or analysis.

Challenges Facing College Leaders

While inequity and bias in analytics have been widely publicized in recent years, the ways these issues surface within colleges and universities are unpredictable for a few reasons. A significant source is the convergence of multiple major developments in higher education. Some have been unfolding for decades and others have emerged more recently. The erosion of the traditional financial model and the changing composition of student bodies have been challenges for years. Both issues accelerated in the aftermath of the Great Recession of 2008-2009 and have continued to intensify during the COVID-19 pandemic. In response to renewed calls for racial and social justice in 2020 and 2021, colleges and universities have become more attuned to the varied needs of diverse students, including adult and continuing education students. This awareness prompted many institutions to get serious about using data more broadly to serve an increasingly diverse student population better. As a result, demand for information outpaced institutional capacity to provide it. This difficulty is magnified by a lack of planning, a lack of resources, and by campus politics.

Senior campus leaders often make the mistake of deferring the development of a culture of evidence and advanced analytics capabilities. Without a strategy that maps out and coordinates the actions that will take an institution to its ideal state, campus leaders will not be able to determine whether progress is being made. In a context where the adoption of advanced analytics is becoming an increasingly urgent priority, faculty, staff, and shared governance bodies will have little tolerance for ambiguity and an inability to measure success.

The task of developing and scaling out the use of advanced analytics is further complicated by the collision of resource constraints and expectations about how resources will be distributed. Even if clear plans and strategies are developed and articulated, there are fewer resources to go around at most colleges and universities. At a time when leaders are talking about doing more with less, even mentioning the possibility of reallocating scarce campus resources to advanced analytics is risky. If a president announces that the procurement of new tools, software, and analysts to improve student success and help promote academic quality is a top priority, the chair of the faculty senate might respond that the institution should just hire more full-time faculty instead of relying more heavily on adjuncts. If a provost tells the dean of advisement that data analytics will make the jobs of advisors easier, the dean might respond that an easier solution would be to hire advisors and commit to lowering their caseloads. In such a context, it can be hard to generate enthusiasm for investing in the resources needed to develop a robust advanced analytics system.

Eventually, lack of a strategy, resource constraints, and campus politics will collide with growing pressures from stakeholders, such as the board or the state legislature, to use big data and some leaders will feel compelled to outsource analytics to external vendors. This creates a cycle in which an institution never begins to wean itself away from external solutions and what should be a short-term option that facilitates the development and emergence of a mission-critical capability becomes dependency. Leaders are left to hope that out-of-the box predictive analytics solutions will do what they claim to do well enough for their campus, although that outcome is far from guaranteed. Vendors need to generate revenue and often tightly guard their algorithms and models to protect their intellectual property. Without a complete understanding of the data or the analytics techniques a vendor is using, it can be nearly impossible to know whether the solution they provide is biased in some unintentional or hidden way against the college and the students it serves.

This uncertainty is compounded by the growing frequency of leadership transitions. Often when a president or a provost leaves an institution, the momentum toward a mature data analytics state abruptly halts, then atrophies. Continuous attention to the development and monitoring of a data analytics system is required if an institution wants to keep current, so a year of idling ultimately causes regression. When a new president or provost is chosen, it usually is not because they promised to maintain the legacy of their predecessor. New senior campus leaders face pressure to improve their effectiveness quickly, so they often jumpstart new efforts rather than build on old ones. This approach hurts morale and creates tension and entrenchment among the stakeholders who are invested in the previous effort to build data analytics capacity on campus, and often the quick solution is a turn to outsourcing.

None of these challenges related to bias should deter a college leader from making every effort to use advanced analytics to improve student outcomes, promote academic excellence, and ensure that the financial model of the institution is sustainable. It is vital to be aware of various forms of bias, how they can be introduced, and what effects they can have on efforts to use data. They underscore the importance of a well-maintained and well-monitored data governance system regardless of who the senior campus leaders are, because a well-maintained and well-monitored data governance system creates an adaptable infrastructure that can integrate new goals and aspirations. When data analytics solutions are planned and sustained properly, they can inspire a college by generating excitement about preventing discrimination and bias. So what can college and university leaders do to help their campuses endorse and embrace the development of a mature in-house system of advanced analytics?

Steps toward Creating an Institution Powered by Analytics

Making the shift toward an analytics-powered college or university is not a sprint. It is also not as simple as purchasing cutting-edge technology. Such a major shift requires a steady hand. College and university leaders can follow a sequence of steps that will increase the probability that their campus will embrace and maintain a mature, well-functioning data analytics system.

Create a Plan for an Equity-Driven Approach and Deputize a Leader

Senior campus leaders should embed the importance of quality, unbiased data in their vision for the campus and in broader organizational goals. A plan for using data and advanced analytics should focus on both realizing its full potential and reducing the risks and unintended consequences of bias in data, methods, and people. The plan should focus on the ideal end state and the potential value that will be generated by realizing it.

Someone needs to lead the creation and implementation of such a plan. More and more, colleges are creating new executive roles or repurposing existing executive roles to establish chief strategy officers and chief data officers who oversee the development of this work. The people who occupy these new roles are often charged with taking inventory of advanced analytics capabilities and related pilot projects, mapping the universe of data assets and their multidimensional flows, noting organizational and technological silos, and assessing the campus's strengths and areas for improvement. They also typically focus on translating analyses into actions that benefit students and create smarter campuses.

Anusha Dhasarathy and colleagues have identified the steps an institution can take as it begins to build a data analytics system.[28] One way is to start with a specific use case that offers cross-functional value to the college. Identifying this case begins with a process of data discovery, including where data reside, who owns them, and how they are accessed. Once the process of discovery has concluded, data can be reviewed, cleaned, and integrated, which opens the door to analysis. After value has been demonstrated, the process can be automated with a focus on quality, completeness, and fitness for its intended use. At this point, the data relevant to this specific use case can be codified through the college's governance framework and scaled out to relevant users for routine use. Through this process, colleges can create a model for using advanced analytics to improve student outcomes, promote cost savings, and increase institutional effectiveness.

Send Signals that Foster Campus Alignment

Although many colleges are using advanced analytics in some form, these projects tend to be isolated within a specific unit or department, and as a result they usually fail to achieve maximum impact. The benefit of designating a leader who is charged with developing a strategy for building a data plan is that these isolated pockets of excellence can be aligned in cross-functional ways to move the entire college forward. This alignment must occur across institutional leadership at all levels. While the president and the cabinet need to be in agreement about how to deploy advanced analytics, that is not adequate. Deans, department chairs, mid-level managers, influential faculty, student leaders, and governance bodies all need to be involved. A recent McKinsey study of analytics use in the business sector noted that companies that are viewed as leaders in analytics adoption were almost twice as likely as other companies to have middle managers who strongly supported the adoption of analytics and understood its future importance.[29] The president and the provost have particularly important roles in setting the tone by communicating the importance and value of analytics and the cabinet has a responsibility to deliver this message repeatedly and clearly. A strong signal of support from senior leaders helps increase the chances that deans, department chairs, influential faculty, student leaders, and governance bodies will support the effort.

Creatively Invest in Capabilities

When institutions are facing resource constraints, it can be difficult to invest in data analytics experts, new technology, and better data. Hidden costs, including cultural and political capital, are also associated with creating better and more integrated data. These types of capital are difficult to accumulate and easy to spend down. Still, the resources need to come from somewhere, and in recent years college leaders have created innovation and reinvestment funds with resources freed up through greater efficiencies and cost savings or the creation of new profit centers, whether those are new academic programs, new credential types, or new auxiliary services. Earmarking a proportion of innovation and reinvestment dollars for strengthening analytics capacity can help presidents and provosts sidestep difficult conversations.

Taking similarly creative approaches to the reconfiguration of staff lines can be a way to adapt a college's work force without increasing it. Other talent investment strategies that can help turn a college's vision for the use of advanced analytics into reality include integrating the expertise with analytics in job descriptions for current employees and new hires, providing staff with the professional development they need to participate in data analysis well, and holding staff accountable for doing so. Luckily, colleges and universities often already have staff who are experts in analytics methodologies. While it is highly unlikely that the average campus will be able to invest in dozens of analytics professionals, it is entirely possible to create a deep bench of analytics experts by identifying faculty and staff with the necessary skills and providing them with incentives (e.g., overtime pay, release time, reduced teaching load) to focus on adopting and scaling out more sophisticated analytics capabilities.

Build Foundations and Blend Functions

Data governance is essential for the successful realization of an advanced analytics system. Key steps include creating and empowering a data governance committee, identifying champions and celebrating accomplishments, and developing a framework for measuring success. Once these steps are complete, senior campus leaders can begin to build on that foundation by tapping experts in institutional research, information technology, academic affairs, budget and finance, and other areas who have the right set of skills and capabilities and charging them with prototyping and scaling out more sophisticated analytics techniques. Campus leaders may encounter resistance to this strategy because department heads and office managers tend to think of the data they have created as their property. In addition, division chiefs might balk at the idea of their staff being used for a new set of priorities that they were not generated within the division. Presidents and provosts are uniquely able to cut through this reaction by either formally creating a cross-divisional team or by developing an analytics advisory board that has broad authority to bring together diverse teams that focus on using and continuously improving the use of predictive analytics, machine learning, and artificial intelligence on campus.

Take Clear Steps to Show Your Embrace of Analytics

Presidents, provosts, and their cabinets have to practice what they preach. Too often, they fall back on old habits and rely on consensus, instincts and experience instead of evidence from data analytics when they make decisions. To limit such behaviors, a decision-making framework that privileges analytics in the most important cross-divisional functions is crucial. At the same time, it is important to make room for lived experience, which is also a rich source of data.

This process starts by articulating clear roles for the president's cabinet, which should include defining it as an advisory body. The next step involves identifying and tiering the cross-functional issues (e.g., student success, equity, strategic finance, academic quality and integrity) based on the impact they have on the institution. Next, a matrix that provides a decision-making framework should be developed. It should include the degree to which a decision is made by one individual or a group of people and note the kinds of advanced analytics that will be used to make decisions. Over time, examples of the value derived from this analytics-informed decision-making matrix will help ensure that the biggest decisions are made from a body of strong evidence.

Conclusion

If used ethically and effectively, advanced analytics has immense potential. Senior campus leaders should proceed carefully, however, given the cautionary tales that have surfaced from early adoption efforts and lessons from other sectors. Creating a plan that takes into consideration the promise and peril of advanced analytics and minimizes the risks to students who have traditionally been poorly served by higher education can help ensure that the reality of advanced analytics matches the rhetoric surrounding it. As with most aspects of higher education, successful execution often boils down to how change is managed and implemented.

Chapter 9

Implementation and Planning

College and university leaders must consider both strategic and operational dimensions as they build out the ability of their campus to use data well. Leaders must have a clear understanding of key concepts of data and advanced analytics, what data and analytics can do for their institution, the dangers associated with bias and improper design, and a commitment to nurturing throughout the college a culture of evidence. All of these elements are highly visible, and well-informed leaders know they are making progress toward a data-informed college when they see it. Forces and processes that are less visible contribute to the realization of an ideal state, however. The most important relate to how change is managed and implemented.

Steps toward Reaching the Ideal State

Senior campus leaders need to be able to answer the question, Where do you want to go? Clearly identifying the outcomes associated with a commitment to data and advanced analytics makes it possible to map the journey, operationalize clear goals and metrics, and deputize and empower leaders in each area to deliver results. Wherever possible, use existing efforts and artifacts, such as institutional plans, self-studies, and available data sets, as you identify and communicate the ideal state. That helps generate buy-in by eliminating the perception that using data and advanced analytics will be yet another new job to add to an already unmanageable list of tasks. The opposite is in fact true: using data analytics will help make people's jobs more manageable. Building on the progress faculty, staff, and students have already made honors their efforts and inspires enthusiasm.

Communicating your vision for the ideal state should be done in its comprehensive form but also in bite-sized pieces that are tailored to those who will be tasked with using data in specific ways. For example, at Lehman College, a Strategy, Policy and Analytics function was created to define and implement a vision for using data based on a formal charge from the president that included the following tasks:

- Cultivate a culture of evidence-based decision-making, continuous improvement and assessment, and anticipation by empowering the campus through data analytics.
- In partnership with institutional technology, lead an ongoing conversation about data governance.
- Create a networked analytics function that over time would serve in a change leadership role.
- Use a variety of data sources and advanced analytics to create a series of analytics products that are designed to help the college achieve its stated goals.

In response to this charge, the following vision and mission statements were created to guide these efforts.[1]

- Vision: The Strategy, Policy, and Analytics function will become a national model for using evidence to facilitate transformational change and student success in the service of equity.

- Mission: The Strategy, Policy, and Analytics function will engage the campus in an evidence-based process of continuous improvement.

The broader goal of promoting transformational change, student success, and equity was frequently communicated to members of the cabinet, who partnered with Strategy, Policy, and Analytics to translate what these priorities meant to each of their respective divisions. For example, administration and finance could work to create savings and cost efficiencies that could be reinvested in student success, academic quality, or digital infrastructure. Enrollment management could work through college governance (e.g., the college senate, relevant faculty bodies, enrollment management committees) to deprioritize standardized test scores in admissions without sacrificing rates of student persistence and completion. The registrar began to realign course scheduling practices to intersect with student preferences for when they came to campus and the availability of facilities. Faculty were partnered with each other so they could identify opportunities for pedagogical improvement, such as flipped classrooms or jumbo courses. Advancement crafted a compelling evidence-based story to attract funders and position the college well with state and local legislators.

Understand the Actual State of Your Campus

Knowing the ideal state helps institutions understand where they want to go, but that is only half the picture. College leaders must also understand what the current conditions are. The process of learning what the current state of data use is must be designed well and be focused on improvement, otherwise key constituents may come to the table unwillingly because they will be worried that providing information about what data they have and how they use it will work against their interests. However, this step is important. A thorough review of the institution's strengths and opportunities for growth is how campus leaders can gain an understanding of what need to happen for the institution to reach the ideal state they have envisioned.

Some colleges bring in external parties to facilitate this activity, while others prefer to keep the process in house. Both approaches have benefits and drawbacks. Bringing in external parties (e.g., consultants, association experts) to conduct the analysis ensures that the findings have a degree of credibility. External parties rarely know the lay of the land, however, and internal stakeholders can exploit this vulnerability. Hiring external professionals can also be cost prohibitive. On the other hand, if an internal group is deputized to lead this exercise, they may lack an understanding of patterns and trends throughout higher education. They know what they know, which is usually the institution where they work. That will usually mean that they will view how the institution operates through a subjective and optimistic lens. Both approaches present unique challenges that college leaders can minimize through a sound design for the process.

Regardless of who the president or provost enlists to conduct this analysis, it is best done quickly and thoroughly and with a bias toward a big-tent approach. It may be difficult to glean perspectives from as many campus stakeholders as possible in a tight window, but the initial lift pays off in the long term because people have input and feel heard. Some people will react to the strategy of jump-starting efforts to use data with skepticism, so the buy-in gained through an inclusive approach is valuable.

The analysis should include multiple components. Michael Barber, Nickolas Rodriguez, and Ellyn Artis have created a detailed list of the steps needed to conduct a successful analysis of a college's ability to deliver on its aspiration.[2] The review of campus resources results in specific recommendations to help the college move from point A to point B. These recommendations are shared in an initial report and in a more formal report that gives senior campus leaders a series of recommendations that are designed to remove the barriers to creating a data-enabled campus. In recent years, associations such as the National Association of System Heads have helped develop frameworks for reviewing the institutional research functions of public colleges and universities. While these frameworks are more narrowly focused than institution-wide efforts to use data and advanced analytics effectively, they offer a baseline for how a review could be conducted.[3] Once leaders receive the recommendations from the campus review, they need to determine whether to move forward on them. When they choose to do so, presidents and provosts are signing up to build structures and invest resources to ensure the success of the effort.

Build a Core Team and Enlist Champions

Once a president or provost has clearly articulated how college data will support broader institutional goals, the college can assess where current capacities are in relation to where they need to be. This kind of review fills in the blank space that often exists between an unvarnished view of the current reality and the vision for an ideal culture of evidence. At that point, campus leaders must determine who will lead and manage the effort. The simple answer is everyone, but distributed leadership in decentralized models often leads to stalled efforts. A leader needs to be deputized and a core team needs to be built.

The president needs to tap one person that Michael Barber describes as a "delivery leader," the process and operational lead, to see the work through.[4] Barber offers a detailed description of such a leader: "The head of the delivery unit needs to believe in the mission, love data and graphs, be loyal to the boss and excellent at building relationships with politicians and officials."[5] In higher education, a delivery leader will probably come from the pool of senior administrative and academic leaders.

After an individual is appointed to lead the college's efforts to use data well and build a culture of evidence, an implementation team needs to be built to manage and support the work. This team will play multiple roles. The most important one is turning a campus leader's aspiration for data use into reality. Implementation teams work best when they are designed with two organizational features in mind: the fact that campus data tends to be siloed and the fact that higher education institutions are decentralized and often underresourced. The team should be cross-functional to facilitate data integration and draw from existing capacity. Over time, especially as the team generates value, the implementation team should evolve into a structure that is integrated into the budget. If that does not happen, the team stands little chance of becoming sustainable or successful. Finding these resources can be difficult, and if or when they are found, college leaders should expect some pushback against drawing money from established units to create a new one. Although higher education institutions like to either stay as they are or grow in a direction they are familiar with, in the modern world they need to learn to be agile. Building an implementation team focused on using data well is a good way to start.

An implementation team focused on building a culture of evidence has other important responsibilities. The team works across divisions to identify opportunities to demonstrate positive impact and deliver important early wins. From these efforts, a clear series of initial goals will emerge that will build toward a data-enabled institution. These goals are created in partnership with the units that will serve as laboratories for using data differently and more comprehensively. Implementation teams also establish a sense of routine data use, focus on data integration opportunities, create an expectation that progress toward the ideal state of using data will be transparent, and set a positive tone that celebrates progress and troubleshoots problems that emerge along the way. They build organizational capacity by identifying the necessary skills, competencies, toolkits, and frameworks and designing workshops and resources that help create an informed and confederated model of data use. Much of this process relies on the ability of the team to guide the process of managing change, which is ultimately an exercise in communication and engagement. Without an implementation team that focuses on these important roles and resources, adoption of new data practices is likely to be minimal even when a college leader says they want everyone to use data better.

By themselves, implementation teams can only do so much to promote adoption. Champions and momentum are needed throughout the institution in order to keep efforts moving along. Malcolm Gladwell famously described the process of adoption that successful ideas go through, noting that such ideas need to reach a tipping point, and use of data at scale on a college or university campus is no exception.[6] Early in the process, it is likely the case that only a few people will embrace the notion that timely, accurate, relevant, and integrated data could be used in positive ways to boost equitable student outcomes and make the institution fiscally more healthy. With time, vision, support, and nudging, a culture of evidence can reach the tipping point and begin to take hold. A vision for data use and a leader and team charged with realizing it are not enough. Every college that is trying to use data better and more broadly also needs a wide coalition of champions to nudge the practice forward over time in many large and small ways.

This coalition of champions will likely include the institutional research director, the chief information officer, and other principals who hold the keys to the most important silos of data, but the most influential champions will likely be faculty members, advisors, other staff members, and students who share the will to move forward. It also helps if champions have distinct assets to contribute, and leaders may have to look carefully to recognize them. Tucked away in some far corner of the campus there might be a director of student success initiatives who has somehow gained access to information from data sets such as degree audits, the enterprise resource planning system, and the learning management system that in practice do not talk to one another well. A director of first-year student initiatives might have data on patterns and trends in student success that no one else can seem to find and an uncanny ability to convey this information to deans and department chairs. An underappreciated department chair with a golden heart and an inability to say no might have largely unknown data skills and a unique ability to help folks see that things could be done better. The chair of the student senate, who has the ear of the student body, can play a role. These are the campus community members who have unique abilities and resources, and they should be prioritized as senior leaders in a coalition of champions. They can build the road that gets a college from the current reality to the ideal state. Once they are enlisted as champions of the effort to use data, the college can begin its analytics journey.

Understand the Task at Hand

It is vital to understand the barriers that stand in the way of moving a campus away from the uncoordinated use of data and toward a more integrated and intentional model. From the start, an organized approach is vital. Together, the delivery lead, the implementation team, and the coalition of champions can take the first steps toward realizing the better and broader use of data at the college. These steps include conducting a qualitative and quantitative feasibility study that helps lay out the path of least resistance that has the greatest odds of success, works to learn what the drivers of and barriers to success are, formulates a plan of action to scale out what works and overcome what does not, and determines a process for continuous analysis and improvement. This process is how a college will "get better at getting better," as Bryk and colleagues say.[7]

Every effort to use data better begins as a messy business. Over time, things become clearer and more organized. The takeoff is usually murkier than the landing. To start, senior campus leaders, the delivery lead, the implementation team, and the coalition of champions have to sit down together and figure out what on earth they are going to do. The first few meetings should identify metrics—some quantitative and others qualitative, some focused on institutional effectiveness and others more geared toward operationalizing the plan. This mixture helps keep the implementation team focused on important college priorities such as student success and equity, strategic finance, academic quality and renewal, and the implementation milestones that are required to create a culture of evidence. Those milestones might look like this: formation of a data strategy, creation of a data governance plan, major integration of data silos, and provision of training and professional development.

These metrics indicate whether and where the college is succeeding in its efforts to use data better and more broadly. At this point, the implementation team will begin to realize that pragmatic choices may need to be made about developing a measurement framework. There are gold-standard metrics that fit perfectly with measuring if the effort is successful. If they are easy to access, all the better, but often they are not, and it may take substantial time, effort, and energy to get them. Then there are the metrics that are imperfect but far easier to obtain and require substantially less capital to get. Once a set of metrics has been chosen, defined, collected, and shared, a process for reviewing them that honors perspectives of diverse campus constituents, including the implementation and the coalition of champions, should be created. Sharp spikes or drops usually mean that something is off with the data that needs to be investigated and remedied. These issues can usually be explained away by changing a definition, migrating a system, cleaning up coded data, integrating overlooked data, or addressing technology issues. If these issues are not the reason for the outliers, then further analysis and scrutiny are warranted. If something seems off, then the implementation team needs to engage campus constituents in unpacking why outliers in performance may be present. For example, a large jump in the proportion of transfer credits accepted for each student may be explained not by a change in practice but by an adjustment that was made to a process that was previously flawed.

Once metrics that reflect college priorities and implementation milestones have been vetted, they can be used to track performance. This process includes creating benchmarks that can be used to compare progress toward campus goals and implementation within and across divisions, schools, and departments. Particularly in the early phase, it is important to promote trust in the data. For that reason, lowering barriers to accessing and understanding data should be prioritized using a scorecard, a dashboard, or a daily report. In an ideal world, these artifacts would come with explanations of what they mean and instructions on how to use them. Creating and communicating key metrics with guidance about how to use them helps unlock the collective brain power of the college to improve performance. This activity is analytics in its simplest form: using data to conduct analyses that prompt evidence-based, equity-driven actions and help create a better and more sustainable college.

Eventually, new metrics will need to be created. That is a good thing because it reflects progress. When the time comes to do create more metrics, the delivery leader, the implementation team, and the coalition of champions will begin the process anew.

Building an Implementation Plan

Every college has a strategic plan. Some use theirs and others let theirs gather dust on a bookshelf somewhere. Whether the creation of a strategic plan is perfunctory or not often boils down to the existence of an implementation plan. The same can be said for a data plan. Having a data plan without an equal focus on implementation will have a negative impact on a college's analytics journey.

Implementation plans are the connective tissue that link an institution's aspiration to use data with the work that needs to be done to achieve the vision for the campus. Key considerations begin with taking stock of existing plans for data use and integration. It may take time to identify and compile this information because it tends to be disorganized and hard to understand or is known only by a handful of college elders who selectively pass knowledge from person to person through thumb drives, cloud accounts, or oral tradition. Aggregating this information will be a revealing process. Existing plans and previous attempts to use data tend to offer insights into how to move such efforts forward successfully and how not to. These details will inform how the implementation team makes its plan.

Implementation plans do have some commonalities. When they are done well, they illustrate how an institution's aspiration or vision for modern data use gets turned into a series of goals that translate into strategies and, ultimately, actions. Take for example, the implementation plan for achieving the vision and mission created at Lehman College. Table 9.1 presents the framework of the plan. Although it looks relatively straightforward, a lot of coordination had to happen to achieve the ideal state.

Once developed, the framework provides a comprehensive overview of the desired end state and the path to get there. In addition to the framework, implementation plans often include important milestones and checkpoints and detailed timelines that emphasize the next three to six months. Based on the metrics that have been identified, data are tied to the goals, strategies, and actions identified in the plan. Implementation plans typically identify the relevant actors (e.g., people or units), the steps and interactions that need to occur, and the timing of these efforts. They identify connections between goals and strategies and measure their overall impact. They are reinforcing cycles of assessment and continuous improvement.

While implementation plans share common themes, no two are exactly the same because the rewards and risks of using data

TABLE 9.1. *Framework for developing an implementation plan, using data at Lehman College*

Ideal State: The college will develop a strategy, policy, and analytics function that will become a national model in service of equity that will use evidence to facilitate transformational change and student success.

Goal 1: The college will successfully modernize its data infrastructure by integrating distinct data sources.	Goal 2: The college will develop real-time reporting capabilities that provide actionable information.	Goal 3: The college will scale out a federated model of data use that empowers faculty, staff, and students in the use of evidence.	Goal 4: The college will create and sustain a data governance and utility body that is focused on creating a culture of evidence.	Goal 5: The college will implement advanced analytics platforms while taking appropriate measures to minimize risk, bias, and inequity.

Prioritization of high-impact strategies: 3–5 priority strategies for each goal.

Empowerment and accountability: each strategy needs a leader charged with making progress.

Actions and improvement: the strategy lead will map major activities, take actions based on evidence, and measure outcomes.

better differ slightly for each institution. A good implementation plan should outline what they are and include recommendations for reaping the rewards and mitigating the risks. The opportunities generally include better student outcomes, a more sustainable institution, improved practices related to accreditation, better assessment, and a more vibrant research and innovation ecosystem. The risks are fairly straightforward, too. People might not want to share data. Faculty might become entrenched in their opposition to the process. Tensions between institutional research and institutional technology might flare up. Expectations and norms regarding shared governance might get violated. There may be insufficient time, will, and money to reach a tipping point of adoption. Unexpected discontinuity in leadership may disrupt or derail the plan. The road from point A to point B will not be straight, and on each campus it will meander in different directions. Implementation plans need to reflect that uniqueness.

Getting into the Habit of Using Data Routinely

The implementation process will require many meetings. Efficient and targeted meetings that focus attention on the matter(s) at hand and are clearly connected to the totality of a college's efforts will respect people's time. Successful implementation hinges on sitting down and discussing what works and what does not. Good routines during meetings provide a structured platform for conversation and action in service of both the larger goal and the more granular strategies, objectives, and actions that determine whether a plan will succeed or fail.

Meetings among key stakeholders should focus on specific measures of progress toward the ideal state and the goals and strategies that will move a campus forward. Meetings should happen regularly and offer a minimum set of standards regarding their frequency and amount of time spent on each topic, the inclusion of data, and open discussion of how best to move forward. Meetings should also focus on actions and accountability and propel the process forward as much as they reflect on progress made to date. They should include the usual participants but be flexible enough to include other people who are not part of the team who bring diverse perspectives based on specific experiences or responsibilities. Meeting should be open to people other than the implementation team, to a degree.

Preparation is one of the key ingredients to a successful meeting. The delivery lead and the implementation team should create a calendar of priorities based on the sequence of events that was identified in the planning phase. The academic calendar provides some general benchmarks. Fall brings the census date and winter and spring focus on applications. In late spring, attention often turns to the successful closeout of the fiscal year and the beginning of the next one. Everything else tends to fall in the spaces between. For each meeting, key metrics should be at the ready to help the group come to consensus about whether a sufficient degree of progress has been made. Before the meeting, it is important to brief stakeholders who will attend or who are responsible for the elements being discussed. No one likes surprises, and if the team leader does not touch base with each participant, key qualitative data may be missing at the meeting that would help the team determine whether a specific group or person has made progress. A pre-meeting brief is common courtesy.

Meetings should be used to scrutinize the progress being made toward the implementation of goals, strategies, and objectives. This involves creating a process for identifying challenges and creating solutions. When a challenge seems too big to solve, it usually can be deconstructed into more manageable pieces that members of the implementation team can handle.

For example, often when a campus begins the process of integrating data, it quickly realizes that data is highly siloed. This is a systemic problem that cannot be solved by one person. An implementation team meeting that is properly structured can solve many dimensions of such an issue. The process first requires an understanding of why siloed data exist. One of the issues has to do with the culture of the institution: people are skeptical about sharing their data and see data as something they own. Another issue is technological: different systems do not communicate well with one another and creating bridges is difficult. There are numerous other issues, but armed with a series of smaller challenges, the implementation team can determine why these issues are present. Once the team understands the reasons why data is siloed, solutions that will integrate data can be prioritized based on their magnitude and their impact on achieving the ideal state and the capacity of the institution to effect meaningful change. Solving problems with a high order of magnitude that have an adverse impact is a good place to start.

To summarize, it is important for an implementation team to hold regular meetings. When those meetings are organized with intentionality, they can add value instead of wasting time. Meetings are important for tracking progress in building a culture of evidence and for modeling the use of data in beneficial ways. Over time, gains made in these areas will make big problems go away.

Maintaining Progress

Forward progress usually comes in small measures because it is a major undertaking with many moving parts. Senior campus leaders and the implementation team can take several actions to nudge movement toward data analytics forward.[8] Leaders can help the campus maintain a clear focus on building a culture of evidence despite the day-to-day issues that emerge and divert attention. In fact, leaders can use new issues as an opportunity to reinforce the need for better data and charge the delivery lead and implementation team them with working to solve them. The team's success in finding solutions will elevate their profile on campus and operate to convince more people to buy in to the project.

Over time, the enthusiasm and optimism surrounding the creation of a culture of evidence can wane. Naysayers will look for a chance to dig in their heels. Campus leaders can maintain momentum by providing the right rewards and incentives. A good strategy is to listen to skeptics and enlist them in identifying solutions to major challenges. Presidents and provosts can promote a positive culture of critique by allowing for contrarian perspectives. By delaying judgment about the arguments contrarians make until all the evidence has been presented, senior campus leaders can model what it means to be influenced by better data and insights. When leaders model this behavior repeatedly over time, it begins to positively shift the college's mindset because stakeholders will see data as a tool that has real influence.

Finally, people appreciate acknowledgement for their good work. Saying "thank you" is perhaps the least expensive and most impactful way to build a data-informed culture. Leaders can celebrate success in big and small ways. For example, sponsoring an annual summit on student success focused on the intersection of data and technology is an effective practice that blends internal and external perspectives on data use. It also gives faculty and staff a platform for showcasing success stories, workshopping challenges, and being recognized for going above and beyond the call of duty.

Common Implementation Challenges

The implementation of analytics and the creation of a culture of evidence within a college or university is not a linear process. There are several reasons for this. At the macro level, many institutions operate with an incomplete understanding of implementation. The prevailing view of implementation is that it requires only a one-time, labor-intensive effort.

The reality is that successful implementation is a never-ending process that includes multiple phases, including acquiring and developing new analytics tools, data sources, or software; implementing new capabilities, which includes migration, transition, and adoption; scaling out new practices; and renewing data and analytics and a culture of evidence on an ongoing basis. Few institutions have codified the importance of implementation by creating a position, let alone an office, that is charged with ensuring the integrity of all phases of implementation. Instead, institutions take a piecemeal approach to the implementation of specific projects. Senior leaders launch task forces or committees, which usually consist of faculty and staff who lack the resources needed to successfully manage implementation. As a result, the launch of a new analytics platform is often celebrated as the end point, not a beginning. After the celebration ends, no one remains to nurture the use of new data or tools and they never reach achieve their full potential. Frustration mounts because the tool never reaches its full value and people question the wisdom of the initial investment.

Failure to Communicate the Purpose of Aspirations

Newly defined aspirations serve to galvanize the college community. Aspirations often include a series of high-level commitments that will help the campus community reach a lofty ambition that holds the promise of greater visibility, a stronger reputation, greater enrollment, and new revenues that can be reinvested into the academic core. They can also lack specificity, and the longer it takes to articulate the details, the more likely it is that people will fill in the blanks on their own. When this happens, a senior college leader can lose control of the message. Optimism can give way to uncertainty and a narrative can develop instead. Things can stagnate. This is especially true when data and analytics are boldly proclaimed to be a key part of an institution's solution to myriad and new challenges. Campus leaders should develop a clear value proposition for using data, including how it will be used in support of the aspiration and the payoff for campus stakeholders who are willing to embrace the journey. The lack of such clarity serves as a wedge issue that individual actors can use to halt buy-in and progress.

Same Words, Different Meanings

Clearly articulating a data-informed aspiration and its key components are just the first steps of a long journey. Ample opportunities exist for efforts to move toward data analytics to get tripped up. One danger is that people have different understandings of what the terms data and analytics mean. The false assumption of a shared language may seem like a minor detail at first, but the longer it takes to realize the error, the bigger the risks become. Given the strategic importance of using data in response to the evidence imperative facing colleges and universities, initial discussions should invite questions that will give the leaders of the project opportunities to clarify meanings and goals. Clarifying conversation is just as vital to the success of an analytics initiative as the sources, methods, and measures taken.

Design Solutions for Power Users, not Champions

Having senior college leaders champion the use of data is a good thing. However, champions and power users are very different. Analytics efforts are frequently designed through the eyes of senior leaders, even though they have little time to roll up their sleeves and immerse themselves in the many granular issues related to platforms, tools, or analysis. Aggregated patterns and trends can hide differences across disciplines, departments, and organizational units. They can also mask the equity gaps and structural deficits that plague colleges and universities nationwide. This significantly limits the utility of data and can aggravate concerns that the tools are designed to serve the interests of a president, dean, or provost rather than the needs of departments, programs, and administrative offices.

Ways to Address Challenges

Make the Resources Needed to Use Data Permanent

Efforts to implement analytics and create a culture of evidence begin to fail when resources dry up. Colleges and universities are struggling to maintain organizations in their traditional forms in the context of a newly volatile financial model. Even if the initial phases of new analytics initiatives result in consensus about the path forward and enthusiasm about shifting to evidence-based decision-making, plans to permanently fund and codify this new endeavor can get bogged down by the harsh new financial realities on college and university campuses. There must be a commitment across the organization to implementing data analytics and creating a culture of evidence. That commitment needs to include a financial plan that supports the endeavor to shift to data analytics. In some cases, dedicated resources means dedicated staff and in others it requires a plan to cover the recurring costs associated with partnering with external vendors. Money for incentives should also be included to foster an ongoing process of renewal that leads to the scaled-out adoption of data analytics. Without funds, even the best-laid plans for the use of data and analytics will eventually sputter.

Continuously Improve and Interrogate Your Approach

Many senior college leaders judge the success of the implementation phase of a plan to shift to data analytics and a culture of evidence based on whether or not there are immediate gains, also known as quick wins. This is an incomplete conceptualization of what success looks like. Although early wins are important, it would be naïve to think that they will automatically translate into long-term success and a firmly rooted culture of evidence. It is also true that colleges can experience large gains in traditional indicators of academic momentum and progress by using data analytics and still have miles to go in their analytics journey. A properly designed implementation plan appropriately frames early gains as a positive sign that even more can be done if data are used properly and if the institution learns from what has worked and what has not. The better a college or university becomes at recognizing areas for improvement, the less likely it is to reinforce inequity and the more likely it is that data users will recognize the forms of bias that can emerge in each stage of implementing analytics and a culture of evidence.

Recognize and Neutralize Lulls in Implementation and Adoption

Campus leaders are often consumed with the crisis du jour and find it difficult to take a long view. Distractions from organizational priorities tend to have detrimental effects on the progress of campaigns to adopt data analytics and develop a culture of evidence. That is an unavoidable reality for senior college and university leaders. The solution is to put structures in place that can quickly identify when there is a lull in implementation and adoption and develop protocols to restore momentum.

Conclusion

Colleges and universities must evolve and become more nimble. Approaching internal and external pressures in traditional ways has not resulted in reliable and ongoing institutional transformation. In the new financial circumstances campuses face, the implementation of a culture of evidence is truly an organizational imperative. Developing the ability to use data to sense and respond to challenges and opportunities institutions face helps colleges address modern demands that will continue to change rapidly. Articulating the ideal state for college data use and developing a data strategy help set the stage, but leaders need to supplement these efforts by committing to effective implementation. Execution of the plan includes appointing a delivery leader and gathering an implementation team whose members are solely tasked with moving the institution to the ideal state of data use. Together with a coalition of champions, this team articulates key goals and strategies, assesses organizational strengths and areas for improvement, and maps how to integrate siloed and uneven data step by step. Over time, if this effort is orchestrated properly, a college or university can become more data-enabled and position itself well for a sustainable future. However, it is important to understand that this journey does not have an end point. A leader's commitment to implementing the institution's plan to move to data analytics includes sustaining and nurturing a culture of evidence.

Chapter 10

Looking Ahead

In recent years, many people have come to perceive higher education as an entrenched structure that is as likely to perpetuate inequity as it is to eliminate it. Despite concerns about whether colleges and universities can remain impactful and effective in their current compositions, many continue to innovate and thrive while doing so. As evidenced in previous chapters, numerous institutions are developing programs and services to meet contemporary student demands, restructure their organizations to withstand financial volatility, and leverage technology and modern approaches to pedagogy to expand their reach and enhance teaching and learning in equitable ways.

Colleges and universities have been approaching a point of inflection for years. The signs have become clear over the last few decades, especially following the Great Recession of 2008-2009, which ushered in austere times. News of strategic mergers and consolidations, a growing annual rate of college closures, and slow gains in outcomes and uneven progress toward equity are the result of the convergence of several external pressures and a stubborn business model that is no longer effective.[1] The COVID-19 pandemic intensified these trends and accelerated the need for transformational change. Faced with perhaps the biggest crisis in modern memory, the entire higher education sector quickly and literally paused operations. In a rare moment of collective consciousness, college leaders from around the country urgently surveyed the landscape and engaged in self-reflection with a singular focus that put the need for change in sharp relief. Put bluntly, many senior campus leaders realized that in order for their institution to be successful, it needed to modernize and operate differently than it had in earlier and less disruptive times. Data and analytics are tools that can help them implement the reforms that will get them where they need to go.

The Higher Education Model Is Changing

In many ways, higher education has become atomized as the composition of student bodies and the needs of students have changed. Students no longer structure their lives around attending college. The changing nature of work and the related need for lifelong learning, advancements in technology, and the emergence of alternatives to traditional colleges have led to a growth in the number of post-traditional students. Students now juggle learning, work, and parenting, among other important responsibilities, every day. They also move from campus to campus, cobbling together courses and credits in pursuit of a hard-earned credential that they hope will result in a better job. They do not view postsecondary education as a linear and timebound experience confined to a single institution or even as what we think of as college. The emergence of new competitors in higher education and the recent surge in alternative credentials is evidence of changing student needs.[2]

Students today are savvy customers with busy lives who increasingly value personalization, convenience, and flexibility over prestige and exclusivity. They want a positive experience and they want to see their voices and perspectives reflected in the services their colleges provide. This desire pertains to academic programs, credit transfers, credit for prior learning, the curriculum, pedagogy, delivery options, advising, and support services. However, many institutions have dug in their heels instead of acknowledging that major structural changes are needed.

Although the need for change did not appear suddenly, events in recent years have accelerated these trends by years and perhaps decades. Institutions and their leaders have suddenly been thrust into an environment they thought would develop years from now. The institutions that have been organizing themselves and investing in infrastructure modernization are best positioned to benefit from the upending of the traditional business model. This chapter provides some key concepts that will help leaders jump-start their institution's efforts to use data and analytics successfully.

For a postsecondary institution to succeed in the next few decades, it will need to invest in the invisible, invaluable infrastructure of data and analytics. It is not too late to begin this process, but now is the time to do so. Early adopters and champions have demonstrated the value that an intentional approach to harnessing the analytics revolution can offer, and a growing number of colleges and universities are beginning their own analytics journeys. The process of moving to campus-wide use of data and analytics is hard work that has no end point. Momentum is difficult to sustain in decentralized organizations made up of domains with different allegiances and agendas. Overcoming internal challenges related to people, processes, data, and technology takes time. These factors can result in uneven or stalled progress. Strong leadership is one of the key ingredients to maximizing a rare opportunity to help evidence-based transformational changes take root.

Advice for Leaders Who Want to Create an Integrated Data System

Beneath the surface, a well-executed data strategy that emphasizes student success, equity, and organizational sustainability acts as a solvent that breaks down silos. Putting time, effort, energy, and money into small programs that can be impactful and disproportionately expensive can create structural budget deficits that are difficult for most institutions to overcome. Integrated data, especially ratios of cost to performance disaggregated by programs, services, and student traits, can reveal opportunities to substantially improve return on investment and free up resources to foster innovation or strengthen teaching and learning.

Start Small and Aim for an Early, Visible Win

The notion of integrating data from siloed units that have sometimes been purposefully kept separate can shake a campus community. Such efforts often remind people of lean and disruptive times. Campus leaders' proclamations that ask people to integrate data are not enough to ensure adoption. Such efforts need to start small and focus on spaces where integrated data are already being used well. These efforts need to be celebrated, and the lessons learned from them should be applied to priority areas based on where college goals intersect with the needs of schools, departments, and chairs and faculty. An early positive approach to data governance and use can yield a stronger, more collaborative, and less combative culture of evidence. For example, integrated data can provide answers to key questions that many campus stakeholders need answers to, such as the definition of what counts as a major or what student-faculty ratio is or what the ideal teaching load would be for the health of both students and the institution. This approach boils down to designing data governance plans that create minimum standards that campus units can customize based on their unique traits. Finance and institutional technology will have different data needs, for example, as will biomedical engineering and social work.

Create a Unique Aspiration for Your Institution that Includes Measurable Milestones

Almost any college or university has a mission and a vision for itself, but few have crafted an aspiration that is clearly measurable. This aspiration will look different depending on the institution. At an elite private research university in a state with few competitors and little external governance, the aspiration may be broad and may address a vibrant knowledge ecosystem with clear targets for graduation rates, undergraduate research participation, research, scholarship and creative activity, and economic impact. An urban public college that began as a normal school and is now part of a governing board system charged with serving historically marginalized populations might set an aspiration to learn the total number of degrees earned, average annual earnings above the per capita income of local counties, calculated increases in tax revenues, and rates of graduates' civic and community engagement. Minority-serving institutions might choose to focus their measurement frameworks on the notion of servingness.[3] Developing clearly measurable aspirations and strategies that are tethered to the distinct identity of an institution has multiple benefits. They provide a differentiated value proposition at a time when many skeptics claim that higher education has become homogenized and they provide clear direction to staff who want to know what they are working toward. Regardless of what the aspiration is, an institution needs good data to achieve it.

Start during Opportune Times

Many efforts to use data fall victim to circumstance. Generally speaking, colleges and universities often react to crises by creating efficiencies. During these emergencies, sweeping back a faculty or staff line, cutting a program budget, or restructuring happens either in conjunction with unknown and imperfect data or is partially and subjectively informed by data in a process that foments distrust and entrenchment. This negative association is tough to remove. Senior campus leaders should not wait until difficult times prompt evidence-based action. Ideally, the process of moving a campus to a culture of evidence will include incentives, shared governance, collaboration, and continuous evolution. Ideal times to start building a culture of evidence include the arrival of a new president or provost or an upcoming accreditation self-study.

Listen First, Then Plan

Colleges and universities develop identities that transcend the tenure of any leadership regime. A new administration brings fresh ideas and perspectives that can help sustain an institution's sense of purpose—if those ideas are introduced as ways to enhance and adapt the mission, vision, and values of the campus. A new president or provost who uses their first days to promote what they accomplished at their former institution will quickly lose favor with campus elders. Instead of asking an entire campus community to adapt to a predetermined measurement framework, college leaders should plan to spend their first few months listening intently. Only then, and only after reflecting on the points of intersection between their playbook and the college's identity, should they make any proclamation about how the campus can improve. Leaders should also spend time with historical documents, self-studies, and senate meeting minutes for clues about what works and what does not and why. This exercise in organizational anthropology generates rich qualitative data that can make or break a data strategy. Any data strategy should be anchored in the distinctiveness of the college.

Create Measures That Meet the Needs of Data Users

In addition to customizing any measurement framework for the unique identity of a college or university, it is crucial to develop measurable objectives that are aligned with the roles individuals have on campus and how those individuals define success. The cabinet needs both the total and aggregated view so they can see where opportunities for improvement exist and identify major deficits based on performance gaps. Department chairs need to understand grade distribution, course fill rates, and major counts. Individual faculty members need to know if students are learning from a particular lecture or module and whether variability exists across course sections both in the present and over time. Advisors need data that help them customize how they talk and interact with students based on whether they are working learners, parents, veterans, or all three. The more a specific a role is, the more granular the data need to be. Aggregates are good for senior leaders; actionable data are good for faculty and advisors.[4]

Align the Data Strategy and Measurement Framework with the Mission of the Institution

Any measurement framework should help the institution realize its full potential in a way that honors its uniqueness. Today, this task can be done only if a plan exists to develop quality data and measures that are designed with the institution's aspirational goals in mind. If instead college leaders choose to trudge along using generic and dusty measures, the institution will probably find itself in the middle of the pack with no characteristics that differentiate it from other campuses. Being mediocre during austere times when students have an unprecedented level of options is a recipe for decline. Although boilerplate approaches to data can help ensure that rates of retention, persistence, and completion improve, customized data strategies shine the light on the areas where a college wants to excel or already excels. This provides opportunities to continuously improve and to create a narrative of a unique value proposition.

Focus on Equity, Student Success, and Organizational Sustainability

Too often, conversations about data, equity, student success, and financial sustainability happen in separate contexts. This approach is counterproductive. It stems from the deep-seated inclination of colleges and universities to remain siloed. A data strategy and measurement framework that homes in on the intersection of important issues serves multiple purposes. Getting better at helping students succeed regardless of who they are, where they come from, or how they go to college helps offset the enrollment volatility that keeps senior campus leaders awake at night. Focusing on student success also has a positive impact on the bottom line and helps keep the lights on and the doors open. Student success and student equity are everyone's business and they are good for business. Data should be used to support the pursuit of ensuring that each student's needs are met throughout their time on campus.

Partner with Supporters Early in the Process

Some stakeholders will try to tamp down efforts to use data because it means doing things differently or they perceive it as a threat to the hierarchy of the institution. Where possible, it is best to avoid engaging at the level of these issues at the outset of a college's analytics journey. Instead, focus on engaging and incentivizing a coalition of stakeholders who are willing to use integrated data. By right-sizing early attempts to use integrated data and strategically partnering with campus constituents, senior leaders will improve the likelihood of success. In addition, focusing on a prototype in the beginning of the journey will minimize initial costs. When positive returns begin to come in, leaders will draw the interest of more stakeholders until eventually the college will reach the tipping point and adoption will reach scale. This strategy is a good way to deal with skeptics with loud voices who can sway the college community away from using data.

Take Advantage of the Full Spectrum of Analytics

Many colleges and universities have been slow to reconfigure themselves to realize the full potential of predictive analytics, learning analytics, artificial intelligence, and machine learning.[5] Artificial intelligence and machine learning in particular can extract valuable information from masses of qualitative data and yield descriptive analyses. Institutions should not lose sight of the value of delivering just-in-time descriptive data. College and university leaders should position their institutions to use the full spectrum of analytics as tools that complement one another. They should also make it a point to identify cross-cutting data projects that will have a disproportionately high impact on rates of student success and equity and the financial sustainability of the institution.

Determine How to Fulfill Demands for Real-Time Information

In recent decades, more frequent periods of volatility have increased the demand for real-time information. This shift has been jarring for traditional data shops on campus that do not have the capacity to respond to the increased volume of request for data. These offices and departments have been molded over the years by a regimented schedule that requires them to produce compliance reports, college surveys, and studies that are designed to meet the benchmarks of peer review. However, there are a few truths to remember. First, college leaders need data when they need it, and they want fine-tuned analyses that show what works over long periods of measuring and monitoring. Second, staff members feel uncomfortable providing this information because there is a higher possibility that the data might point leadership in the wrong direction, perhaps because the instrument is suboptimal or the response rate is too low. Senior leaders need to find ways to provide data shops with the resources to produce real-time data and help staff feel comfortable with the idea of imperfect but operationally useful insights.

Avoid the Peril of Modern Approaches to Analytics

New approaches to analytics, for example artificial intelligence, carry unique risks that can work against the goal of creating an equitable learning experience for all students. These risks include issues with privacy and security, fairness and equity, transparency, communications, quality control, and the use of plug-ins and integrations that can lead to breaches. Unmonitored data can introduce biases that reinforce the structural deficiencies that make it more likely that minoritized and marginalized student populations will continue to experience less success in college. A comprehensive approach to identifying the risks that come with the adoption of modern approaches to analytics can give institutions the confidence that data and analytics are being used effectively.[6] Chris DeBrusk, a partner in a global data management firm, has published recommendations about the steps an institution can take to prevent bias in analytics:

- Be intentional about selecting training data (the data used to build predictive models) to ensure that it doesn't reflect environmental conditions that represent historical bias.
- Root out bias by questioning whether preconceived biases are present in past and current institutional practices and accounting for them in the data and analysis.
- Counter bias in dynamic data sets that may introduce previously unseen biases into modeling activities

- Be intentional about planning new approaches to data collection, analysis, and interpretation before biases become baked into how data are used.[7]

Ensure that Data Is High Quality and that People Use It

A data governance group should be deputized to ensure that all campus data is high quality. This group should continuously identify, anticipate, and resolve current and future risks before they become highly problematic. Chief among these risks are the embedded biases that data, analyses, and people bring to the table. The data governance group should also develop a plan to scale out the use of data and analytics. If data quality is not high and people do not use the data in the system, the massive investments that a college or university makes in their ability to collect and analyze big data will be for naught.

Get Buy-In from Students, the Human Face of Our Units of Measurement

As colleges and universities make inroads in creating the infrastructure that will eventually lead to a healthy culture of evidence, many leaders have begun to frame college data as a university-wide asset of value.[8] This framing, which sits at the nexus of leadership, culture change, and data governance, helps create a shared data space that over time will establish a foundation of timely, accurate, and relevant data that can harmonize decision-making and create the platform for building more advanced analytics. A key part of this process is broad consultation with campus stakeholders, but in the rush to complete the consultation process, leaders can neglect to talk to students, who hold valuable perspectives that leaders need to hear.

The marginalization of student voices has always been problematic, but it was less apparent when colleges focused their use of student data on descriptive data related to academics. As the field of data analytics has advanced and become more predictive and prescriptive, it has come to include analysis related to wrap-around services. This capability has led to the integration of highly personalized data in analytics solutions. However, that practice makes students uncomfortable.[9] Given broader discussions about personal data ownership and agency and concerns about privacy and security, colleges will need to be more intentional about engaging students as equal partners in a good-faith effort to determine what gets measured and what does not. If they listen intently, higher education leaders have an opportunity to create trust between students and the campus by humanizing data and giving voice to the people it represents.

Carefully Consider What Should Be Measured

It can be difficult for senior campus leaders to resist the urge to dive into the deep end immediately and collect, measure, and use all possible data. However, those who pause to consult their college community and build the structures to sustain the discussion can establish trust across the institution, accumulate political capital, and perhaps most important, set the campus on a new course guided by many forms of data. Being proactive will grow in importance in future years because data keep evolving and are becoming ever more personal. This evolution introduces many ethical challenges, and how leaders navigate those challenges will go a long way in determining whether they succeed in building a culture of evidence.

In years past, a lack of access to data and the tools to analyze it constrained institutions to discussions of how best to use historical data to create a limited set of descriptive measures. These conversations usually ended with a deeper—and frustrating—understanding of what could not be measured. The emergence of biometric data, financial information, purchase histories, and information about location and interests means that instead of understanding what cannot be measured, college leaders and their communities need to focus on what should not be measured. Campus leaders must walk a very fine line between creating value for students and the college and being invasive and creating unnecessary risks for all involved. It is essential to determine where that line is.

This need for boundaries has implications for colleges and universities, most of which have expanded their online presence and their reliance on software-as-a-service solutions and next-generation technologies. These cloud-based services are highly integrated with other platforms and collect and connect large amounts of increasingly personal data. It would be very wrong to assume that students do not care about their data and their privacy. Their data can affect their futures. This is crucially important for higher education leaders to consider, given that getting a job is one of the primary reasons why students attend college. Many students go to great lengths to protect themselves by curating and self-censoring their information. They are comfortable with a college or university collecting and using their data for educational purposes but are leery of other applications. Many draw the line at immutable identifiers, such as biometric information, and trust that colleges will consider their interests and well-being before using such data.[10]

In recognition of student preferences regarding privacy and control of their data, colleges need to intentionally structure conversations around the merit and purpose of collecting emergent and increasingly available data. Some key areas for college leaders to consider are discussed below.

Internet of Things Data

Researchers have begun to investigate how data from a wide variety of Internet of Things devices (e.g., smartphones and sensors) can be used to automate the evaluation of student performance and continuously monitor students. Automating evaluation could make it possible to eliminate evaluator bias, free up faculty capacity, and create a highly personalized student experience that promotes academic success and student health and well-being.[11] However, collecting and integrating so much data—spanning participation in community activities or athletic events, academic activity, and behavioral activity—to create composite scores of student performance and satisfaction is a dangerous path to take.[12]

Biometric Data

The use of biometric data in higher education is a controversial topic. In 2020, the University of California, Los Angeles, found itself in hot water when it planned to install facial recognition technology to scan the faces of students to give them access to college facilities.[13] Before the system was installed, the editorial board of the *Daily Bruin* pointed out that using facial recognition technology would violate student privacy, erode trust in administration, and create a hostile campus environment. Students expressed concerns over the possibility of biased and inequitable application of technology and made clear that they believed that the dangers of facial recognition outweighed its contributions to a more secure environment.[14] In the future, particularly given the proliferation of biometric sensors like smartwatches and fitness trackers, colleges and universities may be able to track the number of steps a student has taken, their heart rate, or their precise location. Colleges will need to grapple with whether to use vocal characteristics, retina and iris patterns, gait, and perhaps even DNA sequence data. Given the variation in state laws pertaining to biometric data and the absence of federal law, institutions across the country are likely to choose different paths. Senior leaders must tread cautiously.

Mental Health Analytics

In 2018, the Massachusetts Supreme Judicial Court ruled that the Massachusetts Institute of Technology was not responsible for the 2009 suicide of one of its students. In the years between the student's death and the ruling, eighteen Massachusetts universities wrote a brief in support of MIT that included the statement that "professors, in seeking to protect themselves from liability might go overboard in monitoring students, which could dissuade them from talking to anyone about their problems."[15] The Supreme Judicial Court ruling stated that there may be limited circumstances when colleges could bear responsibility for safeguarding students. Senior campus leaders have come to acknowledge that because students' mental health is a major issue that impacts retention rates and student well-being, the issue needs more attention and more resources.[16] As more data regarding the use of student support services become available, it may be tempting to use this information to protect students. But what would be the ethical cost of doing so? This is an important issue for campus leaders to consider.

External Data

Colleges and universities are institutions of higher learning, not surveillance states. As next-generation digital systems that integrate external data from publicly available data sets become the norm, colleges and universities need to be very thoughtful about what they capture and how they use it to better understand their students. This type of data includes federal data on higher education performance and financial and social media data that can be collected and integrated into traditional forms of student and institutional data. For example, dozens of institutions are known to collect web-browsing and financial data to inform their admissions decisions.[17] Installing trafficking software that recognizes cookies, or small files used to monitor and store information about people, including login information, social media information, browsing history, and financial habits, gives them access to this information.[18] This accumulation of data can lead to the creation of indexes that purport to estimate whether a prospective student is actually interested in attending the college. In this way, colleges and universities are in effect building profiles that they can use to target their recruiting efforts. This practice can disadvantage low-income and minoritized populations because the data inaccurately indicate who is likely to choose their institution. As institutions continue to gather highly personalized information, they often fail to disclose the intent behind their data-capture tools and policies. While prospective students make a phone call or visit a campus to gain information about a college or university without being tracked, the truth is that in a highly digital society, digital engagement is the norm, not the exception.[19] As a result, whether or not a student is offered the opportunity to attend an institution of higher education—and successfully earn a degree—may boil down to whether students clearly understand policies and practices regarding their personal data and its use.

Given the proliferation of highly personalized data, college and university leaders need to ask questions about what should and should not be measured. Many institutions are just beginning a prolonged discovery process focused on the breadth of data that is continuously available. Eventually, this process will enable the higher education professionals to distinguish data that are valuable from those that are worthless. Once this happens, colleges and universities will focus their efforts on data that they deem to be valuable. If this process is properly structured and supported, it will become continuous. It will likely be led by the implementation lead in partnership with the data governance committee.

Be Data Informed, not Data Driven

These considerations underscore the distinction between being a data-informed or data-driven institution. The emergence of big data and advanced analytical techniques will fundamentally change higher education. What remains to be seen is whether institutions will use these tools to create better colleges and universities that remain true to their values or if they will use them to govern decision-making and student behavior to such a degree that the democratic and individual journey of learning will be lost to the tyranny of the algorithm.

A key point that we should all remember is that becoming data driven yields total control to what the data tell us, regardless of whether or not the systems, techniques, or analyses are trustworthy or biased. It is better to be data informed and to remember that the practice of data analytics is equal parts art and science. The collective wisdom of college leadership is a hard-won well of rich data that should not be brushed aside. The stakes are remarkably high. While seeking to extract the full promise of data and analytics is a worthy endeavor, it is also a risky one. Going too far down the road of normalizing specific actions and behaviors through automated nudges may in fact nullify the two things American colleges and universities hold most dear: their distinctive identities and their commitment to equity, opportunity, and upward mobility.

Most important, blind faith in the analytics revolution may lead colleges and universities to sacrifice the individual journey toward learning and self-actualization in favor of getting more people to earn credentials that pad résumés but have lower value. Without constant care and attention, college professionals can find themselves in a position where they follow the findings of an analysis that may or may not contain bias at the expense of quality. The truth is that things are not so binary. Data and analytics are incredibly helpful in giving students the best chance to succeed, and senior campus leaders know how to balance art and science as they used data analytics. Each president and provost, and by extension each institution, must find the right balance for itself.

Conclusion

These are exciting times for colleges and universities. Many institutions stand at the threshold of a new era in higher education.

Senior campus leaders are now navigating a transformation accelerated by the events of the last few years with the goal of emerging as better and more agile institutions. Contrary to popular belief, higher education has yet again adapted in spectacular fashion.[20] Unlike previous evolution eras, this one is largely invisible, it is focused first and foremost on students rather than on structures or professors, and it is built on a backbone of data and technology. The emergence of big data and the analytics revolution has truly transformative potential. How college and university presidents and provosts will approach using data and analytics as a tool to create a more equitable college experience for the students institutions serve is yet to be seen. However, the analytics journey we are collectively embarking on is off to a promising start. By using data well, college leaders can reinforce the distinctiveness of their institutions and honor the higher education traditions of shared governance and liberal education while innovating. They can make higher education better and amplify its capacity to transform the people, communities, economies, and society they have the honor to serve.

Notes

Chapter 1. The Evidence Imperative

1. Janna Quitney Anderson and Lee Rainie, *Main Findings: Influence of Big Data in 2020* (Washington, DC: Pew Research Center, 2012), https://www.pewresearch.org/internet/2012/07/20/main-findings-influence-of-big-data-in-2020.

2. "World Internet Usage and Population Statistics: 2021 Year-Q1 Estimates," World Internet Users and 2021 Population Stats, Internet World Stats, last modified March 31, 2021, https://www.internetworldstats.com/stats.htm.

3. Jeff Desjardins, "How Much Data Is Generated Each Day?" World Economic Forum, April 17, 2019, https://www.weforum.org/agenda/2019/04/how-much-data-is-generated-each-day-cf4bddf29f.

4. Branka Vuleta, "How Much Data Is Created Every Day? (27 Staggering Stats)," Seed Scientific, January 28, 2021, https://seedscientific.com/how-much-data-is-created-every-day. According to Gartner, the Internet of Things (IoT) is "the network of physical objects that contain embedded technology to communicate and sense or interact with their internal states or the external environment." https://www.gartner.com/en/information-technology/glossary/internet-of-things.

5. Keith D. Foote, "Big Data Trends in 2020," Data Topics, Dataversity, January 28, 2020, https://www.dataversity.net/big-data-trends-in-2020.

6. "IDC Forecasts Revenues for Big Data and Business Analytics Solutions Will Reach $189.1 Billion This Year with Double-Digit Annual Growth Through 2022," Business Wire, April 4, 2019, https://www.businesswire.com/news/home/20190404005662/en/IDC-Forecasts-Revenues-for-Big-Data-and-Business-Analytics-Solutions-Will-Reach-189.1-Billion-This-Year-with-Double-Digit-Annual-Growth-Through-2022.

7. "Big Data is Everywhere: 5 Ways It's Used in Your Everyday Life," *Bismart*, n.d., https://blog.bismart.com/en/big-data-is-everywhere.

8. Cathy O'Neil, *Weapons of Math Destruction: How Big Data Increases Inequality and Threatens Democracy* (New York: Crown Publishing, 2016), 27.

9. Joanna Redden, Jessica Brand, and Vanesa Terzieva, "Data Harm Record," Data Justice Lab, updated August 2020, https://datajusticelab .org/data-harm-record; "People," Data Justice Lab, n.d., https:// datajusticelab.org/people.

10. Nathan Newman, "How Big Data Enables Economic Harm to Consumers, Especially to Low-Income and Other Vulnerable Sectors of the Population," Public Comments to FTC, 2014, https://www.ftc.gov /system/files/documents/public_comments/2014/08/00015-92370.pdf.

11. Charlie Campbell, "How China Is Using 'Social Credit Scores' to Reward and Punish Its Citizens," *Time*, January 6, 2019, https://time .com/collection/davos-2019/5502592/china-social-credit-score.

12. Anderson and Rainie, *Main Findings: Influence of Big Data in 2020*, 9.

13. Randy Bean and Thomas H. Davenport, "Companies Are Failing in Their Efforts to Become Data-Driven," *Harvard Business Review*, February, 5, 2019, https://hbr.org/2019/02/companies-are-failing-in-their-efforts-to -become-data-driven; Dina Gerdeman, "Companies Love Big Data but Lack the Strategy to Use It Effectively," Working Knowledge, Harvard Business School, August 21, 2017, https://hbswk.hbs.edu/item/companies -love-big-data-but-lack-strategy-to-use-it-effectively.

14. Ben Miller, "It's Time to Worry About College Enrollment Declines among Black Students," Center for American Progress, September 28, 2020, https://www.americanprogress.org/issues/education-postsecon dary/reports/2020/09/28/490838/time-worry-college-enrollment-declines -among-black-students.

15. Peace Bransberger and Demarée K. Michelau, *Knocking at the College Door: Projections of High School Graduates*, 9th ed. (Boulder, CO: Western Interstate Commission for Higher Education, 2016), https://files.eric .ed.gov/fulltext/ED573115.pdf.

16. Richard Fry and Anthony Cilluffo, "A Rising Share of Undergraduates Are from Poor Families, Especially at Less Selective Colleges," Pew Research Center, May 22, 2019, https://www.pewsocialtrends.org/2019 /05/22/a-rising-share-of-undergraduates-are-from-poor-families

-especially-at-less-selective-colleges. Note: The term Latinx will be used throughout the book because it is a gender-inclusive term for individuals who identify as Hispanic or Latino.

17. Fry and Cilluffo, "A Rising Share of Undergraduates Are from Poor Families."

18. Fry and Cilluffo, "A Rising Share of Undergraduates Are from Poor Families."

19. Ashley A. Smith, "Study Finds More Low-Income Students Attending College," *Inside Higher Ed*, May 23, 2019, https://www.insidehighered.com/news/2019/05/23/pew-study-finds-more-poor-students-attending-college.

20. Reihan Salam, "Why Conservatives Are Turning against Higher Education," *The Atlantic*, August 20, 2019, https://www.theatlantic.com/ideas/archive/2019/08/higher-education-has-become-increasingly-partisan/596407/.

21. Paul Fain, "Varsity Blues, Higher Ed's Image and Federal Policy," *Inside Higher Ed*, March 25, 2019, https://www.insidehighered.com/admissions/article/2019/03/25/democratic-lawmakers-join-chorus-critics-higher-education-engine; Doug Lederman, "Understanding Why Some Colleges Create Economic Mobility," *Inside Higher Ed*, October 31, 2017, https://www.insidehighered.com/news/2017/10/31/elevating-economic-mobility-agenda-higher-education-leaders.

22. State Higher Education Executive Officers Association, *State Higher Education Finance: FY 2019* (Boulder, CO: SHEEO, 2020), https://shef.sheeo.org/wp-content/uploads/2020/04/SHEEO_SHEF_FY19_Report.pdf.

23. State Higher Education Executive Officers Association, *State Higher Education Finance*, 10.

24. State Higher Education Executive Officers Association, *State Higher Education Finance*, 10.

25. Jennifer Causey, Faye Huie, Robert Lang, Mikyung Ryu, and Doug Shapiro, *Completing College: National and State Reports*, Signature Report 19 (Herndon, VA: National Student Clearinghouse Research Center, 2020), https://nscresearchcenter.org/wp-content/uploads/Completions_Report_2020.pdf.

26. Cristobal de Brey, Lauren Musu, Joel McFarland, Sidney Wilkinson-Flicker, Melissa Diliberti, Anlan Zhang, Claire Branstetter, and Xiaolei Wang, "Indicator 23: Postsecondary Graduation Rates," in *Status and*

Trends in the Education of Racial and Ethnic Groups (Washington, DC: U.S. Department of Education, 2019), https://nces.ed.gov/programs /raceindicators/indicator_red.asp.

27. Jennifer Ma, Sandy Baum, Matea Pender, and CJ Libassi, *Trends in College Pricing 2018* (New York: The College Board, 2018), https://research .collegeboard.org/pdf/trends-college-pricing-2018-full-report.pdf.

28. Ma et al., *Trends in College Pricing 2018*, 29.

29. Aida Aliyeva, Christopher A. Cody, and Kathryn Low, *The History and Origins of Survey Items for the Integrated Postsecondary Education Data System (2016–17 Update)* (Washington, DC: National Postsecondary Education Cooperative, 2018), https://nces.ed.gov/ipeds/pdf/NPEC /data/NPEC_Paper_IPEDS_History_and_Origins_2018.pdf.

30. Aliyeva, Cody, and Low, *The History and Origins of Survey Items*, 8.

31. "Higher Education Research and Development Survey (HERD)," National Science Foundation, last modified January 2020, https:// www.nsf.gov/statistics/srvyherd/#sd; "Delaware Cost Study," Higher Education Consortia, University of Delaware, n.d., https://hec.ire.udel .edu/

32. Jonathan S. Gagliardi, Lorelle L. Espinosa, Jonathan M. Turk, and Morgan Taylor, *The American College President Study 2017* (Washington, DC: American Council on Education, 2017).

33. Anderson and Rainie, *Main Findings: Influence of Big Data in 2020*, 28.

Chapter 2. Demystifying Data and Analytics

1. "The Big Data Industry to 2025—Market Leading Companies Rapidly Integrating Big Data Technologies with IoT Infrastructure," Cision PR Newswire, March 20, 2020, https://www.prnewswire.com/news -releases/the-big-data-industry-to-2025---market-leading-companies -rapidly-integrating-big-data-technologies-with-iot-infrastructure -301026880.html.

2. Alison DeNisco Rayome, "How to Avoid Unrealistic Data Science Project Expectations: 8 Tips," TechRepublic, February 12, 2019, https://www.techrepublic.com/article/how-to-avoid-unrealistic-data -science-project-expectations-8-tips.

3. "What Is Big Data?" Oracle Corporation, 2019, https://www.oracle .com/a/ocom/docs/what-is-big-data-ebook-4421383.pdf.

4. Amir Gandomi and Murtaza Haider, "Beyond the Hype: Big Data Concepts, Methods, and Analytics," *International Journal of Information*

Management 35, no. 2 (2015): 137–144, https://doi.org/10.1016/j.ijinfomgt
.2014.10.007; "What Is Big Data?" 7.

5. Ilkay Altintas and Amarnath Gupta, "Characteristics of Big Data—
Variety," Coursera, n.d., video, 5:12, https://www.coursera.org/lecture
/big-data-introduction/characteristics-of-big-data-variety-oVg4p;
Michael Chen, "Structured vs. Unstructured Data," Oracle Big Data,
October 9, 2019, https://blogs.oracle.com/bigdata/structured-vs
-unstructured-data.

6. Eileen Yu, "Oracle Looks to Clear Air on Big Data," ZDNet, October 4,
2012 https://www.zdnet.com/article/oracle-looks-to-clear-air-on-big
-data/. There are different kinds of unstructured data. Unstructured
repetitive data, such as phone calls, typically have limited value.
Unstructured nonrepetitive data, such as medical records, student
interviews, feedback forms, or emails, are considered to have a high
level of value.

7. Kasey Panetta, "A Data and Analytics Leader's Guide to Data Literacy,"
Gartner, February 6, 2019, https://www.gartner.com/smarterwithgartner
/a-data-and-analytics-leaders-guide-to-data-literacy/.

8. Josh Bersin and Marc Zao-Sanders, "Boost Your Team's Data Literacy,"
Harvard Business Review, February 12, 2020, https://hbr.org/2020/02
/boost-your-teams-data-literacy.

9. Association for Institutional Research, EDUCAUSE, and the National
Association of College and University Business Officers, "Statement:
Change with Analytics," 2017, https://changewithanalytics.com
/statement.

10. "Data and Analytics," Gartner Glossary, Gartner, n.d., https://www
.gartner.com/en/information-technology/glossary/data-and-analytics.

11. "Client Services: Data Analytics at AIR," American Institutes for
Research, n.d., https://www.air.org/page/client-services-data
-analytics-air.

12. Dan Vesset, "Planning Analytics 101: What Is Our Plan?" *Data Analytics
Blog*, June 26, 2018, https://www.prostrategy.ie/fpm-analytics-planning
-analytics-101-what-is-our-plan/.

13. Vesset, "Planning Analytics 101." Note: Scenario planning is the
process of analyzing future possibilities using data and analytics.
Doing so enables senior leaders to plan for and work toward future
states with a clear understanding of the associated impacts and
risks.

14. Dan Vesset, "Descriptive Analytics 101: What Happened?" *Business Analytics*, IBM, May 10, 2018, accessed May 11, 2018, https://www.ibm .com/blogs/business-analytics/descriptive-analytics-101-what-happened.

15. "Advanced Analytics," Gartner Glossary, n.d., https://www.gartner .com/en/information-technology/glossary/advanced-analytics.

16. "Predictive Analytics," Gartner Glossary, Gartner, n.d., https://www .gartner.com/en/information-technology/glossary/predictive-analytics-2.

17. "Predictive Analytics," Gartner Glossary, Gartner, n.d., https://www .gartner.com/en/information-technology/glossary/predictive-analytics.

18. "Predictive Analytics," Gartner Glossary, Gartner, n.d., https://www .gartner.com/en/information-technology/glossary/predictive-analytics. Note: A recommendation engine uses data to generate suggestions to people, often for specific products and services. In higher education, recommendation systems can be used in enrollment management to suggest best institutional fits for prospective students and course suggestions to advance a program of study, among other things.

19. Bryan Alexander, Kevin Ashford-Rowe, Noreen Barajas-Murphy, Gregory Dobbin, Jessica Knott, Mark McCormack, Jeffery Pomerantz, Ryan Seilhamer, and Nicole Weber, *EDUCAUSE Horizon Report: 2019 Higher Education Edition* (Louisville, CO: EDUCAUSE, 2019), https:// library.educause.edu/resources/2019/4/2019-horizon-report.

20. Alexander et al., *EDUCAUSE Horizon Report*; Kelsey Miller, "What Is Learning Analytics & How Can it Be Used?" February 18, 2020, *Graduate Programs*, Northeastern University, https://www.north eastern.edu/graduate/blog/learning-analytics.

21. "What Is AI? Learn about Artificial Intelligence," Artificial Intelligence, Oracle, n.d., https://www.oracle.com/artificial-intelligence /what-is-artificial-intelligence.html#enterprise-use-ai.

22. Satya Ramaswamy, "How Companies Are Already Using AI," *Harvard Business Review*, April 14, 2017, https://hbr.org/2017/04/how-companies -are-already-using-ai.

23. Meghan Rimol, "Understand 3 Key Types of Machine Learning," Gartner, March 18, 2020, https://www.gartner.com/smarterwithgart ner/understand-3-key-types-of-machine-learning/.

24. Larry Hardesty, "Explained: Neural Networks," *MIT News*, April 14, 2017, https://news.mit.edu/2017/explained-neural-networks-deep -learning-0414.

25. Drew Magliozzi and Tim Renick, "A University Leader's Glossary for AI and Machine Learning," *Inside Higher Ed*, July 17, 2019, https://www.insidehighered.com/digital-learning/views/2019/07/17/university-leader%E2%80%99s-glossary-ai-and-machine-learning.

26. Thomas H. Davenport and Nitin Mittal, "How CEOs Can Lead a Data-Driven Culture," *Harvard Business Review*, March 23, 2020, https://hbr.org/2020/03/how-ceos-can-lead-a-data-driven-culture.

27. American Association of State Colleges and Universities Center for Student Success, "Preparation Materials," Student Success Academy, Orlando, FL, June 13, 2019.

28. American Association of State Colleges and Universities Center for Student Success, "Preparation Materials"; Humanitae Advisors, "Institutional Transformation Assessment," n.d., https://ita.co1.qualtrics.com/jfe/form/SV_9odnYlerS7AWHwa.

29. Randy L. Swing, "Forward," in *The Analytics Revolution in Higher Education: Big Data, Organizational Learning, and Student Success*, ed. Jonathan S. Gagliardi, Amelia Parnell and Julia Carpenter-Hubin (Sterling, VA: Stylus Publishing, 2018), xiii–xiv.

30. Daniel de Vise, "U.S. Falls in Global Ranking of Young Adults Who Finish College," *Washington Post*, September 13, 2011, https://www.washingtonpost.com/local/education/us-falls-in-global-ranking-of-young-adults-who-finish-college/2011/08/22/gIQAAsU3OK_story.html.

Chapter 3. Defining an Institutional Aspiration Using Data

1. "Cornell University's 'Any Person . . . Any Study' named nation's best college motto by Magazine," *Cornell Chronicle*, August 6, 2007, https://news.cornell.edu/stories/2007/08/cornells-any-person-any-study-named-best-college-motto.

2. Cornell University, "Cornell University Core Values," n.d., https://www.cornell.edu/about/values.cfm.

3. Kentucky Council on Postsecondary Education, "Council History," n.d., accessed August 15, 2020, http://cpe.ky.gov/aboutus/history.html.

4. Texas Higher Education Coordinating Board, "60x30TX: Texas Higher Education Strategic Plan: 2015–2030," July 23, 2015, http://reportcenter.highered.texas.gov/agency-publication/miscellaneous/60x30tx-strategic-plan-for-higher-education.

5. California State University, "Graduation Initiative 2025," n.d., https://www2.calstate.edu/csu-system/why-the-csu-matters/graduation-initiative-2025/Pages/default.aspx.

6. "Table 326.10. Graduation Rate from First Institution Attended for First-Time, Full-Time Bachelor's Degree-Seeking Students at 4-Year Postsecondary Institutions, by Race/Ethnicity, Time to Completion, Sex, Control of Institution, and Percentage of Applications Accepted: Selected Cohort Entry Years, 1996 through 2012," National Center for Education Statistics, https://nces.ed.gov/programs/digest/d19/tables/dt19_326.10.asp. The graduation rate is defined as completion of the degree within 150% of the standard length of time to earn a bachelor's degree (i.e., within six years) or associate degree (i.e., within three years).

7. "Table 326.10."

8. Enrollment intensity refers to the number of courses full-time and part-time students take in a semester and/or the continuity of enrollment across semesters.

9. Anthony P. Carneavale, Tamara Jayasundera, and Artem Gulish, "America's Divided Recovery: College Haves and Have-Nots 2016", n.d., https://cew.georgetown.edu/wp-content/uploads/Americas-Divided-Recovery-web.pdf.

10. The Hamilton Project, "Lifetime Earnings by Degree Type," April 26, 2017, https://www.hamiltonproject.org/charts/lifetime_earnings_by_degree_type.

11. "SeekUT, "Frequently Asked Questions," n.d., https://seekut.utsystem.edu/faqs.

12. "The Opportunity Atlas," n.d., https://www.opportunityatlas.org.

13. "Quick Facts: Bronx County, NY," n.d., https://www.census.gov/quickfacts/fact/table/bronxcountynewyork#.

14. "90x30," Lehman College, n.d., https://www.lehman.edu/90x30.

15. Lorelle L. Espinosa, Robert Kelchen, and Morgan Taylor, "Minority Serving Institutions as Engines of Upward Mobility," n.d., https://www.acenet.edu/Documents/MSIs-as-Engines-of-Upward-Mobility.pdf.

Chapter 4. Equity and Student Success

1. Jonathan M. Turk, and Morgan Taylor, "Institutional Research in Support of Student Success at Our Nation's Most Diverse and Inclusive Institutions," *New Directions for Institutional Research* 2019, no. 184 (2019): 75–90.

2. Jonathan S. Gagliardi, Lorelle L. Espinosa, Jonathan M. Turk, and Morgan Taylor, *The American College President Study 2017* (Washington, DC: American Council on Education, 2017).

3. Amelia Parnell, Darlena Jones, Alexis Wesaw, and D. Christopher Brooks, *Institutions' Use of Data and Analytics for Student Success* (Washington, DC: National Association of Student Personnel Administrators, Association for Institutional Research, and EDU-CAUSE, 2018), https://www.naspa.org/images/uploads/main /DATA2018_DOWNLOAD.pdf.

4. Association for Institutional Research, EDUCAUSE, and the National Association of College and University Business Officers, *Analytics Can Change Higher Education. Really* (N.p.: Association for Institutional Research, EDUCAUSE, and the National Association of College and University Business Officers, 2017), 1, https://changewithanalytics.com /statement.

5. Sharon Leu and Jackie Pugh, *Reimagining the Role of Technology in Higher Education: A Supplement to the National Education Technology Plan* (Washington, DC: U.S. Department of Education, Office of Educational Technology, 2017), https://tech.ed.gov/files/2017/01/Higher-Ed-NETP.pdf.

6. Leu and Pugh, *Reimagining the Role of Technology in Higher Education*, 7.

7. Louis Soares, Jonathan S. Gagliardi, and Christopher J. Nellum, *The Post-Traditional Learners Manifesto Revisited: Aligning Postsecondary Education with Real Life for Adult Student Success* (Washington, DC: American Council on Education, 2017), 11, https://www.acenet.edu /Documents/The-Post-Traditional-Learners-Manifesto-Revisited.pdf.

8. Thomas D. Snyder, Cristobal de Brey, and Sally A. Dillow, *Digest of Education Statistics*, 53rd Edition (Washington, DC: U.S. Department of Education, 2019), 409, table 303.40, https://nces.ed.gov/pubs2018 /2018070.pdf.

9. Rebecca Klein-Collins, Jason Taylor, Carianne Bishop, Peace Bransberger, Patrick Lane, and Sarah Leibrandt, *The PLA Boost: Results from a 72-Institution Targeted Study of Prior Learning Assessment and Adult Learning Outcomes* (Boulder, CO: Western Interstate Commission for Higher Education and Council for Adult and Experiential Learning, 2020), https://www.wiche.edu/wp-content/uploads/2020/10/PLA -Boost-Report-CAEL-WICHE-Revised-Dec-2020.pdf.

10. Margaret W. Cahalan, Laura W. Perna, Marisha Addison, Chelsea Murray, Pooja R. Patel, and Nathan Jiang, *Indicators of Higher Education*

Equity in the United States: 2020 Historical Trend Report (Washington, DC: Pell Institute for the Study of Opportunity in Higher Education, Council for Opportunity in Education, and Alliance for Higher Education and Democracy of the University of Pennsylvania, 2020), http://pellinsti tute.org/downloads/publications-Indicators_of_Higher_Education _Equity_in_the_US_2020_Historical_Trend_Report.pdf.

11. Calahan et al., *Indicators of Higher Education Equity in the United States*, 43.

12. Calahan et al., *Indicators of Higher Education Equity in the United States*, 46.

13. Calahan et al., *Indicators of Higher Education Equity in the United States*, 73, 77.

14. Calahan et al., *Indicators of Higher Education Equity in the United States*, 153.

15. "Racial/Ethnic Enrollment in Public Schools," National Center for Education Statistics, last modified May 2021, https://nces.ed.gov /programs/coe/indicator_cge.asp.

16. "Campus Incidents Involve Academic Freedom vs. Hate Speech," interview with Anya Kamenetz, *Morning Edition*, NPR, November 28, 2019, https://www.npr.org/2019/11/28/783551044/campus-incidents -spark-discussions-academic-freedom-vs-hate-speech.*

17. Susan Svrluga, "U. Missouri President, Chancellor Resign over Handling of Racial Incidents," *Washington Post*, November 9, 2015, https://www.washingtonpost.com/news/grade-point/wp/2015/11/09 /missouris-student-government-calls-for-university-presidents-removal.

18. Alicia C. Dowd, Keith Witham, Debbie Hanson, Cheryl D. Ching, Román Liera, and Marlon Fernandez Castro, *Bringing Accountability to Life: How Savvy Data Users Find the "Actionable N" to Improve Equity and Sustainability in Higher Education* (Washington, DC: American Council on Education, 2018), https://www.acenet.edu/Documents/Viewpoints -Bringing-Accountability-to-Life.pdf.

19. Laura Fingerson and David R. Troutman, "Measuring and Enhancing Student Success," *New Directions for Institutional Research* 2019, no. 184 (Winter 2019): 33–46.

20. Christopher M. Mullin, "Student Success: Institutional and Individual Perspectives," *Community College Review* 40, no. 2 (April 2012): 126–144; Fingerson and Troutman, "Measuring and Enhancing Student Success," 35.

21. Dowd et al., *Bringing Accountability to Life*, 10.

22. Dowd et al., *Bringing Accountability to Life*, 4.

23. "Who Collects Which Postsecondary Data?" Institute for Higher Education Policy, n.d., https://www.ihep.org/wp-content/uploads

/2017/04/uploads_docs_pubs_ihep_toward_convergence_appendix
_crosswalk.pdf.

24. EAB, "Barriers to Student Success," 2019, https://attachment.eab.com
/wp-content/uploads/2019/08/36718-AAF-BarriersStudentSuccess.pdf.

25. Joseph Yeado, Kati Haycock, Rob Johnstone, and Priyadarshini
Chaplot, *Learning from High-Performing and Fast-Gaining Institutions: Top
10 Analyses to Provoke Discussion and Action on College Completion* (Washington, DC: Education Trust, 2014), https://edtrust.org/wp-content/uploads
/2013/10/PracticeGuide1.pdf.

26. Amelia R. Parnell, "The Journey of Analytics," *New Directions for
Institutional Research* 2019, no. 184 (2019): 9–20.

27. Ideas42, *Nudging for Success: Using Behavioral Science to Improve the
Postsecondary Student Journey* (New York: Ideas42, 2016), 47, https://www
.ideas42.org/wp-content/uploads/2016/09/Nudging-For-Success-FINAL
.pdf.

28. Ideas42, *Nudging for Success*, 38.

29. Parnell, "The Journey of Analytics," 17.

30. Rayane Alamuddin, Daniel Rossman, and Martin Kurzweil, *Monitoring
Advising Analytics to Promote Success (MAAPS): Evaluation Findings from
the First Year of Implementation* (New York, NY: Ithaka S+R, 2018), 5,
https://sr.ithaka.org/wp-content/uploads/2018/04/SR_Report
_MAAPS_EvaluationFindings_Year1__04022018.pdf

31. Alamuddin, Rossman, and Kurzweil, *Monitoring Advising Analytics to
Promote Success (MAAPS).*

32. Lauren Pellegrino, Andrea Lopez Salazar, and Hoori Santikian
Kalamkarian, *Five Years Later: Technology and Advising Redesign at Early
Adopter Colleges* (New York: Community College Research Center,
Teachers College, Columbia University, 2021), https://ccrc.tc.columbia
.edu/media/k2/attachments/technology-advising-redesign-early
-adopter-colleges.pdf.

33. Timothy M. Renick, "Predictive Analytics, Academic Advising, Early
Alerts, and Student Success," in *Big Data on Campus: Data Analytics and
Decision Making in Higher Education*, ed. Karen L. Webber and Henry Y.
Zheng (Baltimore, MD: Johns Hopkins University Press, 2020), 181.

34. Renick, "Predictive Analytics," 183.

35. Melissa Blankstein and Christine Wolff-Eisenberg, *Measuring the Whole
Student: Landscape Review of Traditional and Holistic Approaches to
Community College Student Success* (New York: Ithaka S+R, 30, 2020),

https://sr.ithaka.org/wp-content/uploads/2020/09/SR-Report
-Measuring-the-Whole-Student-093020.pdf.

36. Soares et al., *The Post-Traditional Learners Manifesto Revisited*, 7–9.
37. Melissa Ezarik. "COVID-Era College: Are Students Satisfied?" *Inside Higher Ed*, March 24, 2021, https://www.insidehighered.com/news/2021/03/24/student-experiences-during-covid-and-campus-reopening-concerns.

Chapter 5. Strategic Finance and Resource Optimization

1. Yereth Rosen, "Deep Budget Cuts Put University of Alaska in Crisis Mode: 'Grappling with Survival,'" Reuters, July 22, 2019, https://www.reuters.com/article/us-alaska-politics/deep-budget-cuts-put-university-of-alaska-in-crisis-mode-grappling-with-survival-idUSKCN1UH2H0.
2. Gaby Román, "Illinois' Public Universities Have Taken a 48 Percent Funding Cut since 2000," Center for Tax and Budget Accountability, February 26, 2019, https://budgetblog.ctbaonline.org/illinois-public-universities-have-taken-a-48-percent-funding-cut-since-2000-9ee47ac271b2.
3. Gordon Russell, "Special Report: How Startling, Unique Cuts Have Transformed Louisiana's Universities," *New Orleans Advocate*, February 12, 2016, https://www.nola.com/news/education/article_1c7952d6-09bb-5e62-9812-f7099218de47.html; Rich Kremer, "Report: Wisconsin Saw Fourth-Largest Decline in Higher Ed Funding Between 2013 and 2018," *Wisconsin Public Radio*, April 15, 2019, https://www.wpr.org/report-wisconsin-saw-fourth-largest-decline-higher-ed-funding-between-2013-and-2018.
4. Sandy Baum, "State Higher Education Financing Models" (MHEC Policy Brief, Midwestern Higher Education Compact, Minneapolis, MN, 2017), 1, https://www.mhec.org/sites/default/files/resources/mhec_affordability_series1_20170301.pdf; William R. Doyle, Amberly B. Dziesinski, and Jennifer A. Delaney, "Modeling Volatility in Public Funding for Higher Education," *Journal of Education Finance* 46, no. 4 (2021): 563–591.
5. State Higher Education Executive Officers, *State Higher Education Finance: FY 2019* (Boulder, CO: SHEEO, 2020), https://shef.sheeo.org/wp-content/uploads/2020/04/SHEEO_SHEF_FY19_Report.pdf.
6. Doyle, Dziesinski, and Delaney, "Modeling Volatility in Public Funding for Higher Education," 2.

7. John Cheslock and Matt Gianneschi, "Replacing State Appropriations with Alternative Revenue Sources: The Case of Voluntary Support," *Journal of Higher Education* 79, no. 2 (2008): 208–229; State Higher Education Executive Officers, *State Higher Education Finance: FY 2012* (Boulder, CO: SHEEO, 2013), https://files.eric.ed.gov/fulltext/ED540264.pdf.

8. T. Austin Lacy, Jacob Fowles, David A. Tandberg, and Shouping Hu, "U.S. State Higher Education Appropriations: Assessing the Relationships between Agency Politicization, Centralization, and Volatility," *Policy and Society* 36, no. 1 (2017): 16–33, https://doi.org/10.1080/14494035.2017.1290201.

9. Iván Alfaro, Nicholas Bloom, and Xiaoji Lin, "The Finance Uncertainty Multiplier" (Working Paper 24571, National Bureau of Economic Research, Cambridge, MA, 2018), https://www.nber.org/system/files/working_papers/w24571/w24571.pdf.

10. Pew Charitable Trusts, "Western, Southern States Gain Residents the Fastest," Fiscal 50: State Trends and Analysis, November 28, 2013, last modified December 2021, https://www.pewtrusts.org/en/research-and-analysis/data-visualizations/2014/fiscal-50#ind10.

11. United States Census Bureau, "Nevada and Idaho Are the Nation's Fastest-Growing States," news release CB18-193, December 19, 2018, https://www.census.gov/newsroom/press-releases/2018/estimates-national-state.html.

12. NYC Planning, "Population—Current and Projected Populations," n.d., https://www1.nyc.gov/site/planning/planning-level/nyc-population/current-future-populations.page.

13. Catey Hill, "3 Reasons So Many People Are Getting the Hell out of the Northeast," *MarketWatch*, December 19, 2019, https://www.marketwatch.com/story/3-reasons-so-many-people-are-getting-the-hell-out-of-the-northeast-2018-10-20; Emmie Martin, "The 15 US States Where Taxes Take the Most out of Your Paycheck," *CNBC*, April 10, 2018, https://www.cnbc.com/2018/04/10/us-states-with-the-highest-tax-burdens.html.

14. Robin Rudowitz, "Medicaid Financing: The Basics," Kaiser Family Foundation, May 7, 2021, https://www.kff.org/medicaid/issue-brief/medicaid-financing-the-basics.

15. Alison Mitchell, *Medicaid's Federal Medical Assistance Percentage (FMAP)*, CRS Report R43847 (Washington, DC: Congressional Research Service, last modified July 29, 2020), https://fas.org/sgp/crs/misc/R43847.pdf.

16. Christian González-Rivera, Jonathan Bowles, and Eli Dvorkin, "New York's Older Adult Population Is Booming Statewide," Center for an Urban Future, February 2019, https://nycfuture.org/research/new -yorks-older-adult-population-is-booming-statewide.

17. Thomas J. Kane, Peter R. Orszag, and David L. Gunter, "State Fiscal Constraints and Higher Education Spending: The Role of Medicaid and the Business Cycle" (Discussion Paper No. 11, Urban Institute, Washington, DC, 2003), 10, https://files.eric.ed.gov/fulltext/ED476875.pdf. Kane, Orszag, and Gunter found that Medicaid spending in the period 1988 to 1998 explains 80% of the decline in higher education appropriations. In a related analysis, they found that states have taken longer to return to pre-recession levels of higher education funding since the 1990s.

18. Marnette Federis, "Visa Rules Are Restricting the Future of International Students in the US," *The World*, June 20, 2019, https://www.pri .org/stories/2019-06-20/visa-rules-are-restricting-future-international -students-us.

19. Institute of International Education, "opendoors: 2021 Fast Facts," https://opendoorsdata.org/fast_facts/fast-facts-2021/.

20. NACUBO, *A Strategic Blueprint for an Indispensable Association* (Washington, DC: NACUBO, 2019), https://www.nacubo.org/About/Strategic -Blueprint#SP5_Analytics.

21. Lindsay Wayt, *2019 NACUBO Study of Analytics* (Washington, DC: NACUBO, 2019), http://products.nacubo.org/index.php/nacubo -research/2019-nacubo-study-of-analytics.html.

22. Association for Institutional Research, EDUCAUSE, and NACUBO, "About Us," 2017, https://changewithanalytics.com/about-us.

23. Analytics Advisory Group, *Accelerating Analytics: Data Governance for Business Officers* (Washington, DC: NACUBO, 2020).

24. Andrea Ovans, "What Is a Business Model?" *Harvard Business Review*, January 23, 2015, https://hbr.org/2015/01/what-is-a-business-model.

25. Louis Soares, Patricia Steele, and Lindsay Wayt, *Evolving Higher Education Business Models: Leading with Data to Deliver Results* (Washington, DC: American Council on Education, 2016), iv, https://www.acenet .edu/Documents/Evolving-Higher-Education-Business-Models.pdf.

26. Soares et al., *Evolving Higher Education Business Models*, 14.

27. Donna M. Desroschers and Richard L. Staisloff, "Improving College Affordability with New Higher Education Business Models,"

January 2019, https://rpkgroup.com/wp-content/uploads/2020/06/rpk
-GROUP_Improving-College-Affordability-with-New-Business
-Models_Final_for_Release-HR.pdf.

28. Jennifer Ma, Sandy Baum, Matea Pender, and CJ Libassi, *Trends in College Pricing: 2019* (New York, NY: College Board), 12, figure 3, https://research
.collegeboard.org/pdf/trends-college-pricing-2019-full-report.pdf.

29. Maria Anguiano, Paul D'Anieri Matthew Hull, Ananth Kasturiraman, and Jason Rodriguez, *Optimizing Resource Allocation for Teaching: An Experiment in Activity-Based Costing in Higher Education* (University of California, Riverside, 2018), https://www.pilbaragroup.com/wp
-content/uploads/2017/05/UCR_ABC_Whitepaper.pdf.

Chapter 6. Academic Quality and Renewal

1. Jennifer M. Harrison and Sherri N. Braxton, "Technology Solutions to Support Assessment" (Occasional Paper # 35, National Institute for Learning Outcomes Assessment, Urbana, IL, 2018), https://www
.learningoutcomesassessment.org/wp-content/uploads/2019/02
/OccasionalPaper35.pdf.

2. Madeline St. Amour, "A Push for Equitable Assessment," *Inside Higher Ed*, June 25, 2020, https://www.insidehighered.com/news/2020/06/25
/assessment-group-releases-case-study-series-equitable-ways-judging
-learning.

3. Colleen Flaherty, "Forgotten Chairs," *Inside Higher Ed*, December 1, 2016, https://www.insidehighered.com/news/2016/12/01/new-study
-suggests-training-department-chairs-woefully-inadequate-most
-institutions.

4. Walter H. Gmelch, Drew Roberts, Kelly Ward, and Sally Hirsch, "A Retrospective View of Department Chairs: Lessons Learned," *The Department Chair* 28, no. 1 (2017): 1-4.

5. Complete College America, "15 to Finish/Stay on Track," n.d., https://
completecollege.org/strategy/15-to-finish.

6. Valerie Strauss, "Why So Many College Students Decide to Transfer," *Washington Post*, January 29, 2017, https://www.washingtonpost.com
/news/answer-sheet/wp/2017/01/29/why-so-many-college-students
-decide-to-transfer.

7. Education Advisory Board (EAB), *Promoting Timely Degree Completion: Reconciling Student Choice and the Four-Year Graduation Imperative*

(Washington, DC: EAB, 2016), 52, https://eab.com/wp-content /uploads/2019/07/34022_EMF_AAF_Timely_Degree_Completion.pdf.

8. Jonathan S. Gagliardi, "Measuring Entrepreneurship in the Academic Heartland" (PhD diss., State University of New York at Albany, 2012).

9. Marshall Anthony Jr., "Building a College-Educated America Requires Closing Racial Gaps in Attainment," Center for American Progress, April 6, 2021, https://www.americanprogress.org/issues/education -postsecondary/news/2021/04/06/497888/building-college-educated -america-requires-closing-racial-gaps-attainment.

10. Steve Goldstein, "Nine out of 10 New Jobs Are Going to Those with a College Degree," MarketWatch, June 5, 2018, https://www.marketwatch .com/story/nine-out-of-10-new-jobs-are-going-to-those-with-a-college -degree-2018-06-04.

Chapter 7. Creating a Data Governance System

1. "The World's Most Valuable Resource Is No Longer Oil, but Data," *The Economist*, May 6, 2017, https://www.economist.com/leaders/2017/05 /06/the-worlds-most-valuable-resource-is-no-longer-oil-but-data.

2. Analytics Advisory Group, *Accelerating Analytics: Data Governance for Business Officers* (Washington, DC: NACUBO, 2020).

3. Rana Glasgal and Valentina Nestor, "Data Governance, Data Steward-ship, and the Building of an Analytics Organizational Culture," in *Big Data on Campus: Data Analytics and Decision Making in Higher Education*, ed. Karen L. Webber and Henry Y. Zheng (Baltimore, MD: Johns Hopkins University Press, 2020), 123.

4. Risk Based Security, *2020 Year End Report: Data Breach QuickView* (Richmond, VA: Risk Based Security, 2021), 3.

5. "Summary of Findings," in "2019 Data Breach Investigations Report," Verizon, 2019, https://enterprise.verizon.com/resources/reports/dbir /2019/summary-of-findings.

6. Timothy M. Renick, "Predictive Analytics, Academic Advising, Early Alerts, and Student Success," in *Big Data on Campus: Data Analytics and Decision Making in Higher Education*, ed. Karen L. Webber and Henry Y. Zheng (Baltimore, MD: Johns Hopkins University Press, 2020), 184.

7. "About," University of North Texas, Insights 2.0, n.d., https://data.unt .edu/about.

8. Damian Doyle and Kevin Joseph, "Data Governance: Becoming a Data-Informed Institution," *EDUCAUSE Review*, December 8, 2020,

https://er.educause.edu/blogs/2020/12/data-governance-becoming-a
-data-informed-institution.

9. Liz Henderson, "35 Metrics You Should Use to Monitor Data Governance," Datafloq, October 28, 2015, https://datafloq.com/read/35
-metrics-monitor-data-governance/1601.

Chapter 8. The Promise and Peril of Data and Analytics

1. Richard V. Reeves and Dimitrios Halikias, "Race Gaps in SAT Scores
Highlight Inequality and Hinder Upward Mobility," Brookings, 2017,
https://www.brookings.edu/research/race-gaps-in-sat-scores-highlight
-inequality-and-hinder-upward-mobility.

2. Douglas MacMillan and Nick Anderson, "Student Tracking, Secret
Scores: How College Admissions Offices Rank Prospects before They
Apply," *Washington Post*, October 14, 2019, https://www
.washingtonpost.com/business/2019/10/14/colleges-quietly-rank
-prospective-students-based-their-personal-data.

3. Jasmine Park and Amelia Vance, "Data Privacy in Higher Education: Yes,
Students Care," *EDUCAUSE Review*, February 11, 2021, https://er.educause
.edu/articles/2021/2/data-privacy-in-higher-education-yes-students-care.

4. "Improving the Enrollment Process through Machine Learning,"
Ellucian, n.d., https://www.ellucian.com/insights/improving
-enrollment-process-through-machine-learning.

5. "Ivy Tech Develops Machine Learning Algorithm to Identify At-Risk
Students and Provide Early Intervention," Google, n.d., https://edu
.google.com/why-google/case-studies/ivytech-gcp; Melissa Delaney,
"Universities Use AI to Boost Student Graduation Rates," *EdTech*,
May 31, 2019, https://edtechmagazine.com/higher/article/2019/05
/universities-use-ai-boost-student-graduation-rates.

6. Brandon McKelvey, Linda Sullivan, and Diana Pienaar, "Valencia
College and the University of Central Florida" (lecture, U.S. Department
of Education, Washington, DC, n.d.), https://www2.ed.gov/about
/offices/list/ope/predictiveanalyticsslides.pdf.

7. Todd Brann, "University of Kentucky Student Success and Predictive
Analytics" (lecture, U.S. Department of Education, Washington, DC,
n.d.), https://www2.ed.gov/about/offices/list/ope/predictiveanalyticss
lides.pdf.

8. Rebecca Schisler and Ryan Golden, "Mount President's Attempt to
Improve Retention Rate Included Seeking Dismissal of 20-25

First-Year Students," *The Mountain Echo*, January 19, 2016, http://msmecho.com/2016/01/19/mount-presidents-attempt-to-improve-retention-rate-included-seeking-dismissal-of-20-25-first-year-students; Yonette Joseph and Mike McPhate, "Mount St. Mary's President Quits after Firings Seen as Retaliatory," *New York Times*, February 29, 2016, https://www.nytimes.com/2016/03/02/us/simon-newman-resigns-as-president-of-mount-st-marys.html.

9. Schisler and Golden, "Mount President's Attempt to Improve Retention Rate."

10. Susan Svrluga, "University President Allegedly Says Struggling Freshmen Are Bunnies That Should Be Drowned," *Washington Post*, January 19, 2016, https://www.washingtonpost.com/news/grade-point/wp/2016/01/19/university-president-allegedly-says-struggling-freshmen-are-bunnies-that-should-be-drowned-that-a-glock-should-be-put-to-their-heads.

11. Manuela Ekowo and Iris Palmer, "The Promise and Peril of Predictive Analytics in Higher Education: A Landscape Analysis" (policy paper, New America, Washington, DC, 2016), https://na-production.s3.amazonaws.com/documents/Promise-and-Peril_4.pdf.

12. Audrey Murrell, "Big Data and the Problem of Bias in Higher Education," *Forbes*, May 30, 2019, https://www.forbes.com/sites/audreymurrell/2019/05/30/big-data-and-the-problem-of-bias-in-higher-education.

13. James Manyika, Jake Silberg, and Brittany Presten, "What Do We Do About the Biases in AI?" *Harvard Business Review*, October 25, 2019, https://hbr.org/2019/10/what-do-we-do-about-the-biases-in-ai.

14. Katia Savchuk, "Big Data and Racial Bias: Can That Ghost Be Removed from the Machine?" *Insights*, October 28, 2019, https://www.gsb.stanford.edu/insights/big-data-racial-bias-can-ghost-be-removed-machine.

15. Joy Buolamwini and Timnit Gebru, "Gender Shades: Intersectional Accuracy Disparities in Commercial Gender Classification," *Proceedings of Machine Learning Research* 81 (2018): 1–15, http://proceedings.mlr.press/v81/buolamwini18a/buolamwini18a.pdf.

16. Buolamwini and Gebru, "Gender Shades," 1.

17. "9 Common Mistakes that Lead to Data Bias," Open Data Science, May 20, 2019, https://medium.com/@ODSC/9-common-mistakes-that-lead-to-data-bias-a121580c7d1f.

18. Nicol Turner Lee, Paul Resnick, and Genie Barton, "Algorithmic Bias Detection and Mitigation: Best Practices and Policies to Reduce Consumer Harms," Brookings, May 22, 2019, https://www.brookings .edu/research/algorithmic-bias-detection-and-mitigation-best -practices-and-policies-to-reduce-consumer-harms.

19. Craig S. Smith, "Dealing with Bias in Artificial Intelligence," *New York Times*, last modified January 2, 2020, https://www.nytimes.com/2019 /11/19/technology/artificial-intelligence-bias.html.

20. Lee, Resnick, and Barton, "Algorithmic Bias Detection and Mitigation."

21. Robert M. Kaplan, David A. Chambers, and Russell E. Glasgow, "Big Data and Large Sample Size: A Cautionary Note on the Potential for Bias," *Clinical and Translational Science* 7, no. 4 (2014): 342–246.

22. Matt Day, "How LinkedIn's Search Engine May Reflect a Gender Bias," *Seattle Times*, August 31, 2016, https://www.seattletimes.com/business /microsoft/how-linkedins-search-engine-may-reflect-a-bias/.

23. E. A. Spencer, and J. Brassey, "Ascertainment Bias," The Catalog of Bias, 2017, https://catalogofbias.org/biases/ascertainment-bias/.

24. Kaplan, Chambers, and Glasgow, "Big Data and Large Sample Size."

25. Carmen D. Ng, "Biases in Self-Reported Height and Weight Measure- ments and Their Effects on Modeling Health Outcomes," *SSM Population Health* 7 (May 10, 2019): 1–11.

26. Jeff Larson, Surya Mattu, Lauren Kirchner, and Julia Angwin, "How We Analyzed the COMPAS Recidivism Algorithm," ProPublica, May 23, 2016, https://www.propublica.org/article/how-we-analyzed -the-compas-recidivism-algorithm.

27. Cary Funk and Kim Parker, "4. Blacks in STEM Jobs Are Especially Concerned about Diversity and Discrimination in the Workplace," Pew Research Center, January 9, 2018, https://www.pewresearch.org /social-trends/2018/01/09/blacks-in-stem-jobs-are-especially-concerned -about-diversity-and-discrimination-in-the-workplace.

28. Anusha Dhasarathy, Ankur Ghia, Sian Griffiths, and Rob Wavra, "Accelerating AI Impact by Taming the Data Beast," McKinsey & Company, March 2, 2020, https://www.mckinsey.com/industries /public-and-social-sector/our-insights/accelerating-ai-impact-by -taming-the-data-beast.

29. Peter Bisson, Bryce Hall, Brian McCarthy, and Khaled Rifai, "Breaking Away: The Secrets to Scaling Analytics," McKinsey & Company, May 22,

2018, https://www.mckinsey.com/business-functions/mckinsey
-analytics/our-insights/breaking-away-the-secrets-to-scaling-analytics.

Chapter 9. Implementation and Planning

1. Jonathan S. Gagliardi, Gina Johnson, and Amanda Janice Roberson, "Leadership in Enhancing Postsecondary Data Policy to Improve Student Outcomes" (paper presented at the Annual Meeting of EDUCAUSE, Denver, CO, October 31, 2018).

2. Michael Barber, Nickolas C. Rodriguez, and Ellyn Artis, *Deliverology in Practice: How Education Leaders Are Improving Student Outcomes* (Thousand Oaks, CA: Corwin, 2016).

3. Jonathan S. Gagliardi and Jane Wellman, *Meeting Demands for Improvements in Public System Institutional Research: Assessing and Improving the Institutional Research Function in Public University Systems* (Adelphi, MD: National Association of System Heads, 2015), https://www.airweb.org/docs/default-source/documents-for-pages/reports-and-publications/assessing-and-improving-the-ir-function-in-public-university-systems.pdf.

4. Michael Barber, *Instruction to Deliver: Fighting to Transform Britain's Public Services* (London: Methuen, 2008).

5. Michael Barber, "It's All in the Detail: Key Lessons of Delivery in Government," Medium, June 13, 2018, https://medium.com/@michael.barber/its-all-in-the-detail-key-lessons-of-delivery-in-government-5b0d918afdb4.

6. Malcolm Gladwell, *The Tipping Point: How Little Things Can Make a Big Difference* (New York: Little, Brown & Co., 2006), 29.

7. Anthony S. Bryk, Louis M. Gomez, Alicia Grunow, and Paul G. LeMahieu, *Learning to Improve: How America's Schools Can Get Better at Getting Better* (Cambridge, MA: Harvard Education Press, 2015).

8. Steven B. Sample, *The Contrarian's Guide to Leadership* (San Francisco, CA: Jossey-Bass, 2003).

Chapter 10. Looking Ahead

1. Marshall Anthony Jr. "Building a College-Educated America Requires Closing Racial Gaps in Attainment," Center for American Progress, April 6, 2021, https://www.americanprogress.org/issues/education-postsecondary/news/2021/04/06/497888/building-college-educated-america-requires-closing-racial-gaps-attainment; Jonathan S. Gagliardi

and Gina Johnson, "The Evidence Imperative: Reflections on How Volatility and Data Are Reshaping the Relationship Between IR and College and University Presidents," in "Changing Nature and Expectations of Institutional Research," ed. Jason F. Simon and Kara Larkan-Skinner, special issue, *New Directions for Institutional Research* 2020, no. 185-186 (2020): 105-122.

2. Lindsay McKenzie, "At Home, Workers Seek Alternative Credentials," *Inside Higher Ed*, August 10, 2020, https://www.insidehighered.com/news/2020/08/10/surge-alternative-credentials-holds-steady-now.

3. Gina A. Garcia, Anne-Marie Núñez, and Vanessa A. Sansone, "Toward a Multidimensional Conceptual Framework for Understanding 'Servingness' in Hispanic-Serving Institutions: A Synthesis of the Research," *Review of Educational Research* 89, no. 5 (2019): 745-784; Beth Mitchneck, "Conference: Measuring the Success of Institutional Efforts at Hispanic-Serving Institutions," Award Abstract No. 2037922, National Science Foundation, July 30, 2020, updated June 8, 2021, https://www.nsf.gov/awardsearch/showAward?AWD_ID=2037922.

4. Alicia C. Dowd, Keith Witham, Debbie Hanson, Cheryl D. Ching, Román Liera, and Marlon Fernandez Castro, *Bringing Accountability to Life: How Savvy Data Users Find the "Actionable N" to Improve Equity and Sustainability in Higher Education* (Washington, DC: American Council on Education, 2018), https://www.acenet.edu/Documents/Viewpoints-Bringing-Accountability-to-Life.pdf.

5. Dirk Ifenthaler, "Are Higher Education Institutions Prepared for Learning Analytics?" *TechTrends* 61, no. 4 (2017): 366-371.

6. Kevin Buehler, Rachel Dooley, Liz Grennan, and Alex Singla, "Getting to Know—and Manage—Your Biggest AI Risks," McKinsey & Company, May 3, 2021, https://www.mckinsey.com/business-functions/mckinsey-analytics/our-insights/getting-to-know-and-manage-your-biggest-ai-risks.

7. Chris DeBrusk, "The Risk of Machine-Learning Bias (and How to Prevent It)," *MIT Sloan Management Review*, March 26, 2018, https://sloanreview.mit.edu/article/the-risk-of-machine-learning-bias-and-how-to-prevent-it/.

8. Jonathan S. Gagliardi, "Unpacking the Messiness of Harnessing the Analytics Revolution," in *The Analytics Revolution in Higher Education: Big Data, Organizational Learning, and Student Success*, ed. Jonathan S. Gagliardi, Amelia Parnell, and Julia Carpenter-Hubin (Herndon, VA:

Stylus Publishing, 2018), 189–190; Timothy M. Renick, "Predictive Analytics, Academic Advising, Early Alerts, and Student Success," in *Big Data on Campus: Data Analytics and Decision Making in Higher Education*, ed. Karen L. Webber and Henry Y. Zheng (Baltimore, MD: Johns Hopkins University Press, 2020), 184–185.

9. Jasmine Park and Amelia Vance, "Data Privacy in Higher Education: Yes, Students Care," *EDUCAUSE Review*, February 11, 2021, https://er .educause.edu/articles/2021/2/data-privacy-in-higher-education-yes -students-care.

10. Park and Vance, "Data Privacy in Higher Education."

11. Prabal Verma and Sandeep K. Sood, "Internet of Things-Based Student Performance Evaluation Framework," *Behaviour & Information Technology* 37, no. 2 (2018): 102–119.

12. Larry Catá Backer, "Next Generation Law: Data Driven Governance and Accountability Based Regulatory Systems in the West, and Social Credit Regimes in China," *Southern California Interdisciplinary Law Journal* 28, no. 1 (2019): 123–172, https://gould.usc.edu/why/students /orgs/ilj/assets/docs/28-1-Backer.pdf.

13. David Lazarus, "Column: Millions of Faces Scanned without Approval—We Need Rules for Facial Recognition," *Los Angeles Times*, January 29, 2021, https://www.latimes.com/business/story/2021-01-29 /column-facial-recognition-privacy.

14. "Editorial: Implementing Facial Recognition Tech Would Be a Violation of Students' Privacy," *Daily Bruin*, January 29, 2020, https:// dailybruin.com/2020/01/29/editorial-implementing-facial-recognition -tech-would-be-a-violation-of-students-privacy.

15. Katharine Q. Seelye, "M.I.T. Is Not Responsible for Student's Suicide, Court Rules," *New York Times*, May 7, 2018, https://www.nytimes.com /2018/05/07/us/mit-student-suicide-lawsuit.html.

16. Hollie Chessman and Morgan Taylor, "College Student Mental Health and Well-Being: A Survey of Presidents," *Higher Education Today*, August 12, 2019, https://www.higheredtoday.org/2019/08/12/college -student-mental-health-well-survey-college-presidents.

17. Douglas MacMillan and Nick Anderson, "Student Tracking, Secret Scores: How College Admissions Offices Rank Prospects before They Apply," *Washington Post*, October 14, 2019, https://www.washingtonpost .com/business/2019/10/14/colleges-quietly-rank-prospective-students -based-their-personal-data.

18. Emily Stewart, "Why Every Website Wants You to Accept Its Cookies," *Vox*, December 10, 2019, https://www.vox.com/recode/2019/12/10/18656519/what-are-cookies-website-tracking-gdpr-privacy.

19. MacMillan and Anderson, "Student Tracking, Secret Scores."

20. Brian C. Mitchell and W. Joseph King, *How to Run a College: A Practical Guide for Trustees, Faculty, Administrators, and Policymakers* (Baltimore, MD: Johns Hopkins University Press, 2018), 135.

Index

University of North Carolina at Greensboro, 57*t*

University of North Texas, 121-122

University of Wisconsin-Eau Claire, 57*t*

unstructured data, 18

upward mobility, 40, 42

Valencia College, 128

value propositions, 40-44, 41*t*, 43*t*, 158

values, 32-33. *See also* institutional aspirations

vendors, 135

Virginia Commonwealth University, 57*t*

vision statements, 34, 143-144

volatility: case study on, 70-72; crises reactions and, 166-167; data governance systems and, 111-113; economic, 68-70, 119; real-time information demands and, 170-171

web browsing history, 127, 176

West Kentucky Community and Technical College, 58

HIGHER ED LEADERSHIP ESSENTIALS
FROM HOPKINS PRESS

  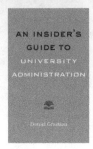 

HOW UNIVERSITY BOARDS WORK

A Guide for Trustees, Officers, and Leaders in Higher Education

Robert A. Scott

An expert guide designed to help university trustees become effective leaders.

HOW UNIVERSITY BUDGETS WORK

Dean O. Smith

An accessible handbook for anyone who needs to understand a university budget—perfect for the non-finance higher ed professional.

HOW TO MARKET A UNIVERSITY

Building Value in a Competitive Environment

Teresa M. Flannery

How can universities implement strategic integrated marketing to effectively build and communicate their value?

AN INSIDER'S GUIDE TO UNIVERSITY ADMINISTRATION

Daniel Grassian

An expert guide designed to help university trustees become effective leaders.

press.jhu.edu

 @JHUPress

 @HopkinsPress

 @JohnsHopkinsUniversityPress